TRANSITION
PARENTHOOD I

A comparative life course
perspective

Edited by Ann Nilsen, Julia rannen and Suzan Lewis

First published in Great Britain in 2013 by

Policy Press
University of Bristol
Fourth Floor
Beacon House
Queen's Road
Bristol BS8 1QU
UK
t: +44 (0)117 331 4054
f: +44 (0)117 331 4093
tpp-info@bristol.ac.uk
www.policypress.co.uk

North American office:
Policy Press
c/o The University of Chicago Press
1427 East 60th Street
Chicago, IL 60637, USA
t: +1 773 702 7700
f: +1 773-702-9756
sales@press.uchicago.edu
www.press.uchicago.edu

British Library Cataloguing in Publication Data
A catalogue record for this book is available from the British Library.

Library of Congress Cataloging-in-Publication Data
A catalog record for this book has been requested.

ISBN 978 1 84742 863 9 paperback

Cover design by Qube Design Associates, Bristol
Front cover: image kindly supplied by www.alamy.com
Printed and bound in Great Britain by TJ International, Padstow
The Policy Press uses environmentally responsible print partners.

MIX
Paper from
responsible sources
FSC® C013056

Contents

List of tables and figures

Tables

Figures

Notes on contributors

Margaret Bäck-Wiklund is professor emerita of social work and family policy at the University of Gothenburg, Sweden. Her research interests are modern family life and parenting. Her current research is focused on the family–work balance. She has been a partner and Swedish coordinator of several European Union (EU) projects. Her many publications include: 'The workplace as an arena for negotiating the work–family boundary: a case study of two social service agencies' (with Lars Plantin, in R. Crompton et al [eds] *Women, men, work and family in Europe*, Palgrave 2007) and *Quality of life and work in Europe. Theory, practice and policy* (Palgrave, 2011), based on the EU study 'Quality'.

Julia Brannen is professor of sociology of the family, Thomas Coram Research Unit, Institute of Education, University of London. She has researched and written about family lives of parents, children and young people in both Britain and Europe and the relation between paid work and family life. She has a particular interest in methodology including mixed methods, biographical approaches and comparative research. Recent books include *Working and caring over the twentieth century: Change and continuity in four-generation families* (Palgrave, 2004), *Coming to care: The work and family lives of workers caring for vulnerable children* (The Policy Press, 2007), *The SAGE handbook of social research methods* (Sage Publications, 2008) and *Work, family and organisations in transition: European perspectives* (The Policy Press, 2009). She is a co-founder and co-editor of the *International Journal of Social Research Methodology*.

Maria das Dores Guerreiro is a professor in the Department of Sociology at the University Lisbon Institute (ISCTE-IUL) (where she coordinates the Master's on Family and Society), and Research Coordinator at CIES-IUL. She has researched and written about families, gender, young generations and work–family balance, both in Portugal and at a European level. Recent publications include *Welfare and everyday life* (Celta, 2009), *Portugal invisível* (Mundos Sociais, 2010), 'Changing contexts, enduring roles? Working parents in Portuguese public and private sector organisations' (in Lewis et al [eds] *Work, families and organisations in transition: European perspectives*, The Policy Press, 2009) and 'Scenarios for the quality of life in the Europe of the future' (in M. Bäck-Wiklund et al [eds] *Quality of life and work in Europe.*

Theory, practice and policy, Palgrave, 2011). She is editor of the journal *Sociologia. Problemas e Práticas*.

Laura den Dulk is associate professor at Erasmus University Rotterdam, Department of Public Administration, the Netherlands. Her main area of expertise is cross-national research regarding work–life policies in organisations in different welfare state regimes. In 2001 she completed her PhD in social sciences on the presence of work–family arrangements in organisations in different European countries. She is co-editor of a number of books: *Work–family arrangements in Europe* (Thela Thesis, 1999), *Flexible working, organizational change and the integration of work and personal life* (Edward Elgar, 2005) and *Quality of life and work. Theory, policy and practice* (Palgrave, 2011). In 2010 she became editor of the international journal *Community, Work & Family*. Current research interests include the role of managers, work–life balance support in the public sector and social quality in European workplaces. She participated in various European Commission research projects: 'Quality of life in a changing Europe' ('Quality') and 'Gender, Parenthood and the Changing European Workplace: Young adults negotiating the work–family boundary' ('Transitions').

Siyka Kovacheva is associate professor in sociology and social policy at the University of Plovdiv (since 1983) and head of the New Europe Centre for Regional Studies in Bulgaria (since 2003). She has held visiting fellowships at the New School for Social Research (1993) and the MacArthur Foundation (1995) at the Kroc Institute, University of Notre Dame, Indiana, US; Tempus/PHARE Programme at the Department of Sociology, Social Policy and Social Work, University of Liverpool, UK (1998); MA WICE Programme, at the University of Wageningen, the Netherlands (2000); and the Thomas Coram Research Unit, Institute of Education, University of London, UK (2005-06). She has been the national coordinator of more than 10 comparative research projects under the fifth and sixth Framework Programme of the EC and other funding institutions. Her research interests are in the field of the social transformation of Bulgarian society, family and intergenerational relations and youth transitions to adulthood. Her publications include *Youth in society. The construction and deconstruction of youth in East and West Europe* (with C. Wallace, Macmillan, 1998), 'Work–life dilemmas: changes in work and family life in the enlarged Europe (*Sociological Problems*, Special Issue, vol IL, 2008) and *Work–life balance: Young working parents between opportunities and constraints* (East-West, 2010, in Bulgarian).

—

Suzan Lewis was coordinator of the 'Transitions' project. She is professor of organisational psychology in the Department of Human Resource Management, Middlesex University Business School, UK. Her research focuses on work–personal life issues and workplace practice, culture and change in different workplace and social policy contexts. She is the co-founder and former editor of the international journal *Community, Work & Family*. Her recent co-authored and edited books include *Work–life integration: Case studies of organisational change* (with C.L Cooper, Wiley, 2005), *The myth of work–life balance* (with R. Gambles and R. Rapoport, Wiley, 2006), *Women, men, work, and family in Europe* (with R. Crompton and C. Lyonette, Palgrave, 2007) and *Work, families and organisations in Transition: European perspectives* (with J. Brannen and A. Nilsen, The Policy Press, 2009).

Ann Nilsen is professor of sociology at the Department of Sociology, University of Bergen, Norway. Her fields of expertise are general sociological theory and methodology and life course and biographical research. She has carried out a number of empirical studies and participated on cross-national teams in studies of young people's transition to adulthood and young Europeans' transition to parenthood. Publications include the co-edited books *Young Europeans, work and family: Futures in transition* (Routledge, 2002) and *Work, families and organisations in transition: European perspectives* (The Policy Press, 2009). She has contributed to methods texts including *The SAGE handbook of social research methods* (Sage Publications, 2008) and *Handbook of mixed methods in social and behavioural research* (Sage Publications, 2010) and published articles in international sociology journals.

Bram Peper is associate professor at the Department of Sociology and at the Department of Criminology, Erasmus University Rotterdam, the Netherlands. His main area of expertise is cross-national research regarding work–life policies and wellbeing in organisations. In 1998 he completed his PhD in social sciences on the genesis of the idea of social problems in modern society. He is co-editor of a number of books: *Flexible working, organizational change and the integration of work and personal life* (Edward Elgar, 2005), an introduction to sociology in Dutch (Pearsons, 2010) and *Diversity, standardization and social transformation* (Ashgate, 2011). Current research interests include the role of managers, wellbeing and depression in European workplaces. He participated in the EC research project: 'Gender, Parenthood and the Changing European Workplace: Young adults negotiating the work–family boundary' ('Transitions').

Lars Plantin is associate professor in health and society at the Department for Social Work at Malmö University, Sweden. His main area of expertise is family sociology with a special focus on fatherhood. In 2001 he presented his thesis, 'Mäns Föräldraskap. Om mäns upplevelser och erfarenheter av faderskapet' ['Men's parenting. On men's perceptions and experiences of fatherhood']. The study was based on a collaborative project between the University of Sunderland in England and the University of Gothenburg in Sweden. He has published various articles on the subject such as 'Talking and doing fatherhood. On fatherhood and masculinity in Sweden and Britain' (*Fathering*, 2003) and 'Different classes, different fathers? On fatherhood, economic conditions and class in Sweden' (*Community, Work & Family*, 2007). He has also published articles and books on themes such as parenthood and the internet, reproductive health and migration, and work and family life.

Nevenka Sadar Černigoj is a senior researcher in the Organisation and Human Resource Research Centre at the University of Ljubljana, Faculty of Social Sciences, Slovenia. Her main areas of research are changing life patterns, gender division of paid and unpaid work, social policies in relation to parenthood, quality of life in various life spheres and women and the labour market. She has participated in several internationally funded European comparative research projects: 'Changing Life Patterns of Families in Europe', 'Childhood as a Social Phenomenon', 'Labour Market Participation of Women in Eastern Europe' and 'Gender, Parenthood and the Changing European Workplace'. She participated in networks of excellence: COST A13, Changing Labour Markets, Welfare Policies and Citizenship – Gender Group and Reconciling Work and Welfare in Europe (RECWOWE, 2005-11). Some of her most recent publications are: 'Social policies related to parenthood and capabilities of Slovenian parents' (with A. Kanjuo Mrčela, *Social Politics*, summer 2011, vol 18, no 2, pp 199-231), 'Societal and organisational contexts of women's careers' (*International Conference – DECOWE*, Ljubljana, 2009) and 'Old rights in new times: the experiences of parents in a Slovenian organization' (in Lewis et al, *Work, families and organisations in transition: European perspectives*, The Policy Press, 2009).

Janet Smithson is a research fellow at the University of Exeter, UK. She has worked on a variety of national and European-funded research projects, using both qualitative and quantitative research methods. Her main research interests include gender and discourse, work–life practices and policies, life course transitions, qualitative methodologies, internet-mediated discourse and communication. Recent publications include: 'Advice, support and troubles telling on a young people's self-harm forum' (*Discourse Studies*, vol 13/4, 2011, forthcoming) and 'Focus groups' (in S. Becker, A. Bryman and H. Ferguson, *Understanding research: Themes, methods and approaches for social policy and social work*, The Policy Press, 2004).

Anneke van Doorne-Huiskes is professor emerita of sociology at the Department of Sociology and ICS Research School of Utrecht University, the Netherlands. Her major research interests lie in the areas of welfare states, labour market and gender, gender and organisation, organisational culture and work–life balance. She has been engaged in the international research project 'Gender, Parenthood and the Changing European Workplace' ('Transitions'), coordinated by Professor Suzan Lewis, Manchester Metropolitan University, UK (2003-06). She participated in 'Quality', an internationally comparative project on quality of life and the work of European citizens, financed by the EC (2006-09). She represented the Netherlands in the EU-Network Family & Work (1995-2001). She participated in 'Defining Family Obligations in Europe: Cross-national research', coordinated by Professor Jane Millar, University of Bath, UK (1994/95). She was a visiting professor at the University of Bath, UK (January-April 1995). She chaired the Social and Behavioural Sciences section of the Netherlands Organisation for Scientific Research (2001-06). Since 1987 she has been a senior partner of VanDoorneHuiskes and partners, a research and consultancy firm in Utrecht, the Netherlands. Her main activities are research in organisations (careers of men and women, mainstreaming gender in human resources management); management development programmes for highly educated women; and participation in European projects on gender ('Equal') and age ('Fair Play').

Acknowledgements

The editors and contributors to this book would like to acknowledge the work of the rest of the Transitions team: Michaela Brockman, Jeanne Fagnani, Lise Granlund, John Howarth, Polona Kersnik, Atanas Matev, Jana Nadoh, Rob Pattman, Christina Purcell, Sevil Sümer and Marijke Veldhoen-van Blitterswijk. They would also like to acknowledge the support of the European Commission for funding the Framework Five project 'Gender, Parenthood and the Changing European Workplace', and the Norwegian Research Council, The Norwegian Non-Fiction Writers Association (NFF) and the University of Bergen for funding meetings and editorial visits which made the writing of this book possible. Gratitude is also due to the organisations that took part in the study and to the parents and managers who gave up their valuable time to be interviewed.

ONE

Introduction

Ann Nilsen, Julia Brannen and Suzan Lewis

Becoming a parent, especially for the first time, marks a major turning point in most people's lives. In this book we explore and examine conditions related to young working parents' decisions and experiences in the transition to the life course phase where they become mothers and fathers, and also the contexts and conditions under which they manage their everyday lives as employees in different national and workplace contexts. All this takes place against a backdrop of current concern across much of the Western world about the demographic imbalance characterised by large birth cohorts nearing retirement age and much smaller birth cohorts in the younger age groups, with consequences for social, economic and cultural spheres of societies. In most countries in the Western hemisphere the birth rate is falling and the mean age at first birth is increasing. During the same period as this demographic shift has taken place, women's workforce participation has increased in the same countries. The two-income family is increasingly the norm, replacing the one-income male breadwinner model that was prevalent across Western Europe and beyond during the first two thirds of the 20th century (Lewis, 2001). Although a relatively short phase historically, the unravelling of the male breadwinner model and its impacts on relationships and structures has been slow and uneven across and within European states (Crompton et al, 2007). This, together with massive global changes in the nature and organisation of paid work, gave rise to what has come to be known as issues of 'work–life balance'.

This book draws on a European Union (EU) research project 'Gender, Parenthood and the Changing European Workplace', henceforth referred to by its shorter name, 'Transitions'.[1] The overall objective of this cross-national study was to examine and compare how young European men and women working in public and private sector workplaces negotiated motherhood, fatherhood and work–family boundaries in the context of different national welfare provisions, family and employer support. The project involved eight countries: Bulgaria, France, the Netherlands, Norway, Portugal, Slovenia, Sweden and the UK. In all countries apart from France, empirical studies were carried out in two phases.[2] The first phase consisted of organisational case studies in a private and/or a public sector organisation. Some of the findings from this phase are discussed in an earlier book (see Lewis et al, 2009). The second phase that is the focus of this book involved biographical interviews with mothers and fathers employed in these organisational settings.

In this second phase we sought to understand experiences of the transition to parenthood from a gendered life course perspective. We were also interested in the gendered experiences of combining waged work and parenting, and parents' work–family strategies as well as the resources they draw on (family, friends, workplace and public policy, especially childcare and parental leave) in the context of different organisational contexts and practices and different national institutions including welfare regimes.

In this book we adopt a comparative focus in each chapter rather than presenting findings from each country separately. This organisation of the book highlights the advantages of a comparative case study design and demonstrates how the approach can tease out elements in the analysis which otherwise might have become part of the 'taken-for-granted' aspects of context which often happens in single country studies. Moreover, it illustrates how the research design transcends the micro–macro divide and shows how individual agency is situated in layers of context that are specific to time and place.

The interviews were carried out in 2003-04, at a time when the economic situation in most of the countries were very different than they are at the time of writing, when most of the world is suffering from the consequences of the economic downturn in the aftermath of the crisis caused by the near collapse of the financial institutions in 2008. At the time of the interviews the future was brighter for most of the interviewees. Indeed, asked about how they thought about the future, both family and job-wise, most had a positive and optimistic outlook. Our findings therefore represent a snapshot of employed parents in specific countries at a particular moment in historical time.

We adopted a life course perspective as an overarching theoretical framework for the Transitions study. Different time modes are interlinked within this research tradition: historical, biographical and everyday time (Hareven, 1982; Elder, 1985; Adam, 1995). Chapter Two focuses on historical time, while biographical time is the main focus in Chapters Four and Five, and everyday time is highlighted in Chapter Seven.

In a life course perspective becoming a parent is discussed as part of a set of events that are involved in the overall transition from one life course phase to another: the transition from youth to adulthood. Although most parents taking part in this study had more than one child, the first transition to parenthood requires special attention since it is one of the most important markers of the adult phase. Many layers of empirical context are brought to bear on the analysis of individual cases in order to give thick descriptions of these to highlight how individual agency and structural circumstances are intertwined in shaping trajectories. The transition to parenthood is discussed in relation to other life course transitions such as school leaving, gainful employment, moving out of parental household and cohabitation/ marriage. The analyses demonstrate that social class, level of education and income are among the important aspects affecting this transition, but that other dimensions such as family support can make the impact of material circumstances different across contexts. The chapters also demonstrate how a notion of adulthood that involves independence from the family of origin must be discussed with reference to differences in national contexts at particular moments in historical time.

The period of youth is shorter for lower educated young people than for those with higher education in that they take on parenthood and paid employment earlier in life (Nilsen et al, 2002). In an earlier study involving Norway, Portugal and the UK (Brannen et al, 2002) we made a distinction between four different types of transition patterns between youth and adulthood:

- *Long period of youth:* those who take higher education but have no financial or other obligations since the family provides housing and covers all other living costs. This is a situation mostly found in Portugal for middle-class young people.
- *Young adulthood,* in which the young move into separate households from their parents but have enough income to provide for themselves through study loans or paid employment. Lifestyle choices are important for those with this type of transition pattern. Such patterns are more frequently found among middle-class young in North Western Europe.
- *Early adulthood* is a third type that describes those who have to take on adult responsibilities early in life by supporting themselves through various low-skilled jobs and have little or no higher education. In some cases they also have children early in life. Their transition is precarious because of lack of resources and support either from the state or from the wider family. This pattern can be found in all countries but is less frequent in a Scandinavian context where welfare state support is stronger.

• The fourth is the *short period of youth*, which is distinguished from the former in that there is some education and support available and young people provide for themselves through vocational training that qualifies them for skilled work. In this type the transition phase is clearly marked off as distinct from adulthood. We have identified this pattern in working-class young people in a Scandinavian context particularly (Nilsen et al, 2002, pp 166-8).

These typologies are constructed from the analysis of qualitative data collected from particular groups in particular places at a particular time by employing a grounded perspective (Brannen and Nilsen, 2002). We should therefore be cautious about their transferability to other empirical evidence (Gomm et al, 2000). This is not least due to institutional differences across national contexts as well as changes in one particular context over time. An example of this is one important marker of adulthood that is mentioned in most youth research: establishing a separate and independent household. In Portugal and Bulgaria, living with parents until marriage has traditionally not been uncommon. However, as the economic changes associated with the transition from communism to a market economy led to a rise in housing costs in Bulgaria, it became very difficult for young families to afford separate housing. Instead, the pooling of resources, housing included, across generations became necessary for many families to make ends meet. With this in mind we only use the typologies of transitions from youth to adulthood to the extent that they are helpful in throwing light on the analysis of the transition to parenthood.

The transition to parenthood is analysed and presented in separate chapters for mothers and fathers. We show that mothers' and fathers' trajectories in education and work are affected differently by parenthood. Women tend to have longer periods out of work when becoming mothers than men when they become fathers. This is a trend in all countries and is not only associated with differences in statutory rights to parental leave, or the differences in length of maternity and paternity leave; nor can it be associated with individual choice alone. Gender differences evident in the shapes of trajectories must also be seen in view of the general institutional arrangements across contexts that offer gendered opportunity structures.

Life course analysis often examines degrees of linearity or non-linearity of the sequence of trajectories. Linearity does not refer to any ideal or standard, only to the sequencing of phases in the life course as these are related to age-specific institutions such as the system of education in a society in question (Elder, 1985; Elder et al, 2006). This reflects the structural aspects of chronological age. However, related to this are the normative expectations of the appropriate timings for certain events and transitions to take place in the life course (Settersten and Hagestad, 1996a, 1996b). As will be demonstrated throughout the chapters in this book, the normative aspect of age is gendered and also varies with social class in different national contexts.

All the cases in this study are parents who were in gainful employment. Moreover, most of them lived with a partner.[3] Had the material included a wider variety of life courses, the variation between them would have been much greater. Many of the higher educated parents in the Transition study, especially in Northern Europe, tend to follow a linear route through upper secondary school and on to higher education, perhaps with a gap year between. The time spent in the system of higher education is notably longer for middle-class young people than those of working-class background with low-skilled jobs. The lifelines (see Chapters Four and Five) also illustrate gendered trajectories: gaps in men's life lines are in some countries related to doing military service after upper secondary school and before higher education; they also show differences in leave schemes for fathers across contexts; and finally they demonstrate very clearly gender differences in working hours. The lifelines thus illustrate how structural circumstances and individual agency interplay to form patterns of trajectories.

We also focus on the experiences and conditions for being a parent in the present, and the different aspects of time relevant for understanding how parenthood and waged work can be combined in everyday life. The circumstances in which parents found themselves are addressed with reference to the accumulation of conditions and experiences of the past and not only those that relate to the present and the ways in which these are shaped by social trends, institutions and public policy at a national level. Comparisons between countries show that, for instance, kin and wider family emerge as particularly important for young parents in Eastern and Southern Europe in the transition to parenthood as well as helping them to manage their busy everyday lives in the present. Historical traditions and culture play an important part here, but equally important are social institutions such as welfare state provisions and housing policies. In Northern Europe there is also a tradition of an ideology of autonomy and independence that sometimes renders invisible the significant amounts of support young people receive from state and family, what we refer to as the 'silent discourses' of interviewee accounts (Brannen and Nilsen, 2005).

In order to create a general contextual framework for the comparative discussions we seek in Chapter Two to give a brief but wide-ranging overview of the historical development in the countries involved in the study, as well as an overview of the life course perspective that necessitates attention to historical context. We concentrate on current discussions in the field of life course research, while also referring to earlier work in this research tradition. It is a difficult and daunting task to give a brief but relevant historical account of 40 years of development of all the countries in the study. The time period covered in the chapter corresponds approximately to the birth year of the oldest of the cohort (1965) included in the study up to the time of the interviews. We decided on an approach that positions the countries in the context of 'clusters' that belong together for historical and institutional reasons: Northern Europe consists of the Scandinavian countries Norway and Sweden, as well as the Netherlands and the UK; there is only the representative of the Southern countries, namely Portugal; Eastern Europe includes the former communist countries that took part in the study – Bulgaria and Slovenia. While there are notable differences between the countries grouped together here, there are still deeper differences that divide the groups of countries than within-group differences, not least with regard to the historical circumstances that characterised the societies into which the interviewees were born. In later chapters, addressing specific research questions, we also discuss institutional arrangements in different countries in more detail, such as access to affordable day care, parental leave schemes and employees' rights under national labour market laws.

Chapter Three discusses methodological issues. The overarching life course framework for the book incorporates a biographical approach, and the methodological design is a cross-national embedded case study. Biographical cases are analysed and discussed as embedded in layers of context where the country is the macro context and the meso level is the workplace. In this chapter we suggest how a comparative approach when applied to such data can help enrich knowledge in general. With this in mind we discuss different notions of generalisability and demonstrate the type of general sociological knowledge that can be gained from contextualised qualitative data that rests on providing thick descriptions of individual cases. The type of knowledge produced suggests the interrelatedness of agency and structure and shows how these concepts may be bridged rather than treated as dichotomous.

In Chapter Four, we undertake comparative biographical analyses of the transition to motherhood in countries selected from each of the three European regions. The chapter adopts a life course perspective and examines the transition to motherhood in relation to other life course transitions such as education and employment. Lifelines are analysed and set in the context of national age-based transitions patterns relating to the system of education, average age at birth of first child and so on. Interpretations and reflections provided by the interviewees about the course of their lives are analysed and compared. Cases also illustrate how the impact of social class and educational level vary across the national contexts. Another important feature is the support available to women in the phase of becoming a new mother. The cases selected show how a cross-national design helps to illuminate aspects of context that would otherwise be among the 'taken-for-granted' elements of biographical accounts. It also demonstrates how, for instance, having a child at an early age, which normatively speaking may be considered a disadvantage at a particular historical moment, can have different impacts on the life course depending on social class and institutional fabric of a specific society.

Chapter Five presents analyses of biographical cases that illustrate differences in transitions to fatherhood. This transition, its timing and the way it is approached by interviewees, is shown to be also strongly related to social class. Those of middle-class backgrounds tend to become fathers later in life than their working-class counterparts, and especially in Northern Europe they have a more 'deliberative' attitude to this transition, thinking and talking about it in relation to other areas of life, and carefully considering the timing of becoming a father. Working-class men tend to approach fatherhood in terms of something that is 'natural' and 'happens to everyone'; compared to middle-class men they do not seem to share the long phase of planning. Together this and the previous chapter demonstrate how parenthood is gendered, and also how gender plays out in different national contexts.

Chapters Six and Seven discuss parenthood in the present and invite different notions of time than biographical time to be addressed. In Chapter Six the range of resources available for working parents is discussed with reference to different national contexts. The chapter draws on material from countries with different labour laws, levels of public and private support for childcare and working hours regulation. It provides cross-national comparisons of types and sources of constraint and support for working parents. While drawing on the case material the chapter conceptualises differences across countries with reference to the *structural characteristics* that provide support or constraints. Thus it provides a further background for the national contexts and what the individual cases are 'cases of', where support for working parents is concerned.

Based on individual case studies Chapter Seven focuses on parents working in similar conditions across countries in terms of occupation and workplaces, and compares mothers employed in a low-status job (care workers in social services) and fathers in higher-status occupations in the finance sector. It explores how parents feel about their lives, focusing on the different sources of support available to them in their particular contexts, and thereby examines the disparity between the conditions of people's lives and how they think about their lives. A temporal lens is employed: the present (2004) of parents' lives is informed by biography but also by contemporary time and orientations to the future. The focus is on the concurrent work–family 'fit' rather than the life course. The chapter suggests how parents are faced with an increasing simultaneity of domains and events in their work, family and children's lives that have different temporalities. This creates a need to multitask and to synchronise what are often irreconcilable timetables leading to feelings of time pressure and a constant state of time pressure and busyness.

In the final chapter (Chapter Eight) we conclude the discussions by focusing on four topics that are central to the book: the issue of time, the importance of context, the salience of class and gender and a final section that discusses future scenarios based on selected case material from previous chapters.

Notes

[1] This acronym was chosen because the overarching research questions we sought to address involved this important life course transition although we did not follow parents as they experienced the transition to parenthood, an approach which would have required a different conceptualisation of transition, for example, as a rite of passage and as a status involving both losses and gains.

[2] In addition, a preliminary phase of the study was a context-mapping phase that did not involve empirical studies.

[3] There were lone parents in the material from each country. One such case will be presented in Chapter Five on the transition to fatherhood. We have not sought to focus on lone parents in particular because this status is for many more often a life course phase than a permanent situation.

TWO

Cross-national comparisons: the history–biography link

Ann Nilsen

Introduction

Different approaches to sociological studies rely not only on a variety of theoretical perspectives and concepts; approaches and perspectives typically also involve the use of sets of concepts that are closely knitted to form coherent frames of understanding. In a discussion of different ways of approaching and discussing motives for action, C.Wright Mills (1963 [1940]) describes how in different times and societies varying vocabularies – sets of terms and concepts – are accepted as standard for explaining motives. He concludes that in order to make sense of these in a sociological way, 'What is needed is to take all these *terminologies* of motive and locate them as *vocabularies* of motive in historic epochs and specified situations. Motives are of no value apart from the delimited societal situations for which they are the appropriate vocabularies' (p 452, emphasis in original). This way of approaching a set of terms and concepts as *vocabularies* can also be helpful for understanding differences in approaches to wider sociological phenomena at a given period in sociological research.

The overarching topic of this book relates to social change. In many contemporary discussions of social change, non-specified terms such as modernity, postmodernity, late modernity, post-industrial societies, information society and so forth are widely used. They have become part and parcel of a standard sociological vocabulary. However, as Anderson (1998) points out in an examination of the term 'postmodernity', its origin was as an aesthetic category in poetry in Latin America in the 1930s and was first used as an epochal category in the works of the British historian Arnold Toynbee in 1954 and referred to as 'the post-modern age' to describe the contemporary historical period in largely negative terms (Anderson, 1998, pp 4-5). Mills (1980 [1959]) also used this term to name the epoch he thought would follow the contemporary modern age with the same foreboding as Toynbee. However, as Anderson observes, in the currently influential writings of Lyotard and Habermas, postmodernity remains vague with reference to time and place – no precise periodisation can be found in their accounts (Anderson, 1998, p 45). Indeed, in all the works Anderson examines in the book,[1] there are problems of demarcation in terms of both time and place (p 78). The vocabulary where postmodernity and its associated terms are most prominent is currently in 'cultural studies', which is very influential in much sociological research (Bonnell and Hunt, 1999), and especially in biographical studies (Denzin, 1989).

Biographical interviews are the main source of empirical material in this book. In our analysis and writings we do not use 'a postmodern vocabulary' because the non-specific quality of these notions renders them of little help in contextualising embedded case study analysis.

For our purposes the main frame of reference is a life course perspective which is based on a different theoretical tradition than cultural studies, and which also makes use of a different vocabulary, one that we find more analytically precise and hence also more helpful for grounding the empirical analyses and interpretations in many layers of context.

The overarching perspective in the Transitions project links biographical and historical time (Mills 1980 [1959]) within the framework of a life course logic (Elder, 1985), thus demonstrating the interrelatedness of structure and agency. This approach has a long history in sociology and employs both qualitative and quantitative methods and data (for an overview, see Nilsen and Brannen, 2010). In the past decade a number of books and articles have addressed the theoretical foundations of life course research and a wide variety of conceptualisations have been developed. Heinz et al (2009) sum up the approach thus: 'As a proper methodological basis for the analysis of social processes, it [the life course approach] denotes an interrelationship between individuals and society that evolves as a time-dependent, dynamic linkage between social structure, institutions, and individual action from birth to death' (p 15). Kohli (2009), discussing different ways of addressing age and the life course, observes that: 'What we have before us is not just a temporal variation of other social givens, or a temporal process, but a *social fact* generated by its own system of rules. In this manner the life course can be conceptualised as a social institution – not in the sense of a social grouping (an aggregate of individuals), but of a pattern of rules ordering a key dimension of life' (p 64). Elder et al (2006) see the life course perspective as a *theoretical orientation*.[2] Drawing on this definition '[they] view the life course as consisting of age-graded patterns that are embedded in social institutions and history. This view is grounded in a contextualist perspective and emphasizes the implications of social pathways in historical time and place for human development and ageing' (Elder et al, 2006, p 4).

As the above definitions suggest, the lives of individuals are embedded in historical time and current contexts. Blossfeld (2009), addressing cross-national comparative life course research, states that '[life course studies] tend to deepen our understanding of cross-national differences when we give a convincing explanation of the impact of institutional and social-cultural conditions on the life course in various nations' (p 281).

In the first part of this chapter concepts and theories related to a life course perspective are discussed in more detail with specific reference to the topic of this book since they provide a *vocabulary*, in Mills' sense, for discussing the transition themes in more precise terms. Moreover, a life course perspective illuminates the intersection of different life course transitions and sets these within historical and institutional frameworks, thus providing a rich backdrop for understanding similarities and contrasts in transitions to parenthood across countries. The perspective, like few others, therefore enables analyses that demonstrate the dynamic relationship between structure and agency.

The second part of the chapter addresses historical and structural features of the countries involved in the Transitions study, and gives an overview of the main macro trends that have been important during the life course of the interviewees. Of necessity this outline is short and lacking in detail at country level. However, such an overview forms an essential layer of context for the analysis and interpretation of biographical interviews and their 'lifelines' (see Chapter Three) that helps to provide 'thick descriptions' of cases. Detailed information about institutional features at country level is provided in the analysis chapters where relevant.

A life course perspective: theoretical and conceptual topics

The history of the life course perspective has its origins in the biographical approach developed by W.I. Thomas and F. Znaniecki in their classic study *The Polish Peasant in Europe and America* (1958 [1918-20]). What sets a life course approach apart from other perspectives in sociology is the insistence on the link between human agency, time and structural features of a society. C. Wright Mills was one of the early sociologists who demonstrated how the biography–history link is an important approach in the discipline (Mills 1980 [1959]). However, as Elder et al (2006) observe, until the 1970s, mainstream sociology 'rarely dug deep into the complexities of life, and too often, in the words of Robert Nisbet (1969 cited in Elder et al 2006), existed in the "timeless realm of the abstract"' (p 5).

Before Elder's groundbreaking study *Children of the Great Depression* (1999 [1974])[3] the more quantitative-oriented life course research in sociology was developed by Cain (1964), Ryder (1965) and also Loewenberg (1971). As Nilsen and Brannen (2010) discuss, although the quantitative and the qualitative approaches to life course and biography in sociology are interlinked, they are not similar, and the latter has been more influenced by the 'cultural turn' in the social sciences than the former.

The concept of *generations*, as discussed by Mannheim (1952) in relation to wider social change, as well as its connotations relating to kin and family, is and was important in this approach. However, because of the multiple definitions of generation (Alwin and McCammon, 2006), the concept of *cohorts* was deemed to offer a more precise reference to the historical placement of individuals and the effects of wider social change on their lives (Ryder, 1965). A birth cohort consists of people who live through the same historical event at about the same age (Ryder, 1965). In Transitions a 10-year birth cohort was selected for individual interviews – those born between 1965 and 1975. They were selected because at the time of the study they comprised the age group who were most likely to have children in the age range we chose to focus on (under 12 years old) and because they were also part of a large birth cohort, being the children of the largest cohort after the Second World War, 'the baby boomers'.

Historical period is another important concept in life course research. In contrast to 'modernity' or 'postmodernity' that refer to vague epochs, historical period refers to historical time in a chronological sense and the institutional fabric of society at a given time period with reference to place. Slow developmental *trends* may distinguish one historical period from another. For the Transitions project some major trends are of particular importance: the demographic shift caused by increased longevity in the population; falling birth rates;[4] the increase in female labour market participation; and the two-income family which is replacing the one-income male breadwinner model (Lewis, 2001).

Historical events may affect individuals differently depending on their *chronological age* and cohort size (Ryder, 1965; Loewenthal, 1971; Riley, 1988; Elder, 1999 [1974]). For the research participants in Transitions one of the most important macro-historical events that has affected their lives was the fall of communism in 1989-90. These events created massive changes, especially in the former communist countries, changes that occurred when the cohort in question was in the life course phase of youth – younger members of this cohort were in their teens and still in education, while the older ones were in the process of establishing households of their own. Other major historical changes in the period include the 'Carnation Revolution' in Portugal that ended 42 years of dictatorship and autocratic rule under Salazar (1932-68) and Caetano (1968-74) (Machado and da Costa, 2000); while for UK research participants the rise of neoliberalism in the 1980s represented a major shift in social as well as economic life circumstances.

Trajectory is another key term. In its wider meaning it refers to a sequence of events in a life course (Elder, 1985). More specifically, a life course is made up of trajectories in different arenas (for example, educational trajectory, employment trajectory and so forth), where circumstances and resources during transitions from one phase to another are important for the course of life as a whole (Elder, 1985).

A closely related concept is that of *transitions*. Significant transitions include the transition between the *life course phases* of childhood, youth and adulthood. Traditionally the transition from youth to adulthood is thought of as a sequence of events that include: completing education, gaining financial independence from the family of origin, setting up a separate household, establishing a long-term relationship with a partner and becoming a parent (Elder, 1985). Hareven (1978) states that particular age groups are problematised and become an issue depending on wider social and economic changes. Hall's book *Adolescence* (1904) is the first instance of discussing the concept of youth as distinct from other phases (Jordan, 1978). Adulthood marks the 'mature individual' (Hareven 1978) and is associated with autonomy and independence from the family of origin. Markers of adulthood change over time with the life course, only becoming clearly structured as a sequence of phases in the West in the 20th century (Hareven, 1978; Kohli, 2009). However, over the past 20 years research has demonstrated that this sequence is not linear, especially as structural changes demand a longer time in education in preparation for gainful employment (Jones and Wallace, 1992; Nilsen et al, 2002; Settersten, 2004, 2009; Benson and Furstenberg, 2007; Kohli, 2009). Some argue that youth as a life course stage is rendered increasingly obsolete since it is being extended indefinitely into both younger and older age groups (Buchman, 1989). Still others focus on a destandardisation of the life course as a whole (Beck and Beck-Gernsheim, 1995; Settersten and Mayer, 1997; Settersten, 2004; Hartmann and Swartz, 2007). Transition patterns between youth and adulthood vary considerably according to social origin and gender (Jones and Wallace, 1992; Irwin, 1995; Hartmann and Swartz, 2007; Lareu and Weininger, 2008) and notably also between countries (Nilsen et al, 2002; Billari and Liefbroer, 2010). *Life course events* refer to important markers such as start of education, marriage/ cohabitation, childbirth etc. Events are thought of in relation to *timing* in the life course with reference to life course phase and age, especially with reference to synchronicity with peers. The social meaning of age also relates to normative expectations of the appropriate time for certain events and transitions to take place (Settersten and Hagestad, 1996a, 1996b; Settersten, 2004). If a woman becomes a mother at a much earlier age than what is considered normative for her social milieu, such asynchronicity with her peers can affect the life course as a whole. There is no single standard transition pattern to adulthood. Quantitative studies show how the timing of events associated with this transition varies and is becoming more complex and protracted (Billari and Liefbroer, 2010), and how subjective feelings of adulthood have changed (Benson and Furstenberg, 2007). At the time of the study the interviewees in Transitions had all taken on full adult responsibilities in the sense discussed above, although not necessarily in a standard sequence – some had experienced the first transition to parenthood in their teens, others had started a family while living with parents or in-laws, and so forth. Such variations are discussed in the cross-national comparisons in the chapters that follow.

Elder et al (2006) systematise what they termed the 'paradigmatic principles in life course theory' in five main principles. Since these sum up the uniqueness of the theoretical underpinnings of life course research and are helpful for understanding the relationship between life course research and general sociology, they are briefly summarised here:

- *The Principle of Life-Span Development:* Human development and aging are lifelong processes.
- *The Principle of Agency:* Individuals construct their own life course through the choices and actions they take within the opportunities and constraints of history and social circumstance.
- *The Principle of Time and Place:* The life course of individuals is embedded and shaped by the historical times and places they experience over their lifetime.
- *The Principle of Timing:* The developmental antecedents and consequences of life transitions, events, and behavioural patterns vary according to their timing in a person's life.

- *The Principle of Linked Lives*: Lives are lived interdependently and socio-historical influences are expressed through this network of shared relationships. (Elder et al 2006, pp. 11-14).

In analyses of life course and biographical data these principles are often not related to individually; more often they form a coherent frame of reference that are taken into consideration throughout the different phases of analysis. However, the third principle, that of time and place, needs addressing specifically in order to provide a deeper and 'thicker' backdrop for the contextualisation of individual lives. Moreover, this principle invites a high level of specificity in describing both time and place features of contextualisation. The next section therefore gives a description of the *overarching* structural and historical characteristics relevant for examining the biographical interviews and lifelines in context. In the individual chapters more details about country-specific institutional frameworks are drawn on where relevant.

Cross-national societies: historical and current contexts

As noted in the previous section an important feature of a life course perspective is that it alerts us to the importance of the opportunity structures provided by national contexts for men and women from different social backgrounds in a particular historical period. In Transitions we sought to make cross-national comparisons of the transition to parenthood for men and women employed in particular organisational settings (Lewis et al, 2009). The focus here is on the life course, and although the organisational setting provides an important part of the embedded frame of understanding, discussions in this book highlight the life course (Chapters Four and Five in particular). In this the cross-national comparisons are an overarching focus of analysis.

Many cross-national studies take welfare state regimes as the main backdrop of comparisons (Hantrais, 2009). Welfare state regimes have been the objects of debates and classification attempts for decades (for some of the feminist arguments in the debate, see, for example, Daly and Rake, 2003, and Sümer, 2009). One of the most influential typologies is that of Esping-Andersen (1990).[5] Three distinct types are identified: the liberal, the conservative (corporatist) and the social democratic welfare state. Although this typology was considered ground breaking on its publication, and is still by far the most cited, it also raised debate and critique (for an overview of the debates from a theoretical viewpoint, see Arts and Gelissen, 2002). For instance both Ferrera (1996) and

Bonoli (1997)[6] brought up the fact that Esping-Andersen's model fails to account for the role of families in Southern European welfare states. Bonoli (1997) also discusses feminist critique against the typology since it does not take into consideration the treatment of women in society (p 355).[7]

However, cross-national studies may have different intentions and purposes and nation itself may be approached in different ways. Kohn's (1987) distinction between four different types of cross-national studies, where the approach to 'nation' varies, is helpful for setting the scene for what type of comparisons a study hopes to achieve: nation as an *object* of study; nation as a *context* of study; nation as a *unit of analysis*; and studies that are *transnational* (p 714). The methodological aspects of cross-national research are discussed more fully in Chapter Three; suffice to say here that in Transitions we adopted a framework that approached nations as *context*. Within nations' borders are social institutions that carry history and agency particular to a place or space, which again must be understood and made sense of as opportunity structures related to individual agency.

Since in the analysis of our biographical material we take as the point of departure the concept of countries as *contexts*, it is important to focus on a wider set of social institutions than welfare state regimes alone. Blossfeld (2009) expands the number of institutional characteristics that are helpful in cross-national life course research and concludes that the system of education, the industrial relations system, welfare state regimes and family traditions are the most important institutional structures for understanding agency within a given society (p 296). Space does not permit an extensive overview of these institutions here. However, based on other research and literature, a broad-brush picture is presented of some key historical changes for the countries involved in this study from the latter half of the 20th century when the older members of the cohort were born. In this the focus is on countries as *context* in a way that provides a 'thick' background for the interpretation of interviews and lifelines.

Before the fall of the Iron Curtain

Hobsbawm (1994) discusses how among historians the period between the 1950s and 1973 is named 'the golden age' or 'the golden years'. He observes:

> [...] it was not until the great boom was over, in the disturbed seventies, waiting for the traumatic eighties, that

observers – mainly, to begin with, economists – began to realise that the world, particularly the world of developed capitalism, had passed through an altogether exceptional phase of its history; perhaps a unique one. (pp 257-8)

'The affluent society' resting on full employment[8] did not become widespread until the 1960s. Institutions such as the United Nations (UN) and the Organisation for Economic Co-operation and Development (OECD) as late as the early 1970s predicted continuous economic growth and a popular belief in economic progress abounded (Hobsbawm, 1994).[9] The situation beyond the then Iron Curtain was different in many ways, but as Hobsbawm notes, the growth rate in the USSR and the whole of the Eastern Bloc was equal to, or faster than, that of the capitalist West. Even if the general affluence experienced by most Western nations was beyond the reach of the majority of the world's population, Hobsbawm saw 'the golden age' as a worldwide phenomenon (Hobsbawm, 1994).

The belief in progress and affluence characterised the societies into which the bulk of our interviewees were born. From the time of the events relating to the 'oil crisis' of 1973 that demonstrated the economic growth's dependence on oil (Hobsbawm, 1994), there was economic turmoil and social unrest in many countries in the West and East alike. Deregulation of capital and right wing political ideas gaining more prominence in the West were also characteristics of this period (Hobsbawm, 1994). However, until the fall of communism and the break up of the USSR in the early 1990s, the Iron Curtain remained, resulting in huge differences in living conditions between people in the East and West.

East of the Iron Curtain

In the Transitions study two countries from the former Soviet Bloc were included: Bulgaria and Slovenia. Although now dissimilar, before the fall of communism they shared some characteristics.[10] As in most Eastern Bloc countries, farming and industry were the most important sectors of the economy in both Bulgaria and the former Yugoslavia, of which Slovenia was at the time a part. The planned economy demanded state ownership of land and manufacturing plants; run by a single party system there were no democratic elections (Hobsbawm, 1994; Kovacheva, 2001).

In these countries much attention was devoted to the youth phase. In the 1960s all countries in the Eastern Bloc followed a Soviet initiative to establish official youth political organisations on the model of Komsomol, where an average of 80 per cent of young people aged 14-28 across the countries were members (Kovacheva, 2001, p 44). State-provided leisure activities and subsidised housing were privileges enjoyed by this age group. The system of education under communism was to prepare new generations to serve in a centrally planned economy. Education was free, school material included, and the quality of education was generally high (Kovacheva, 2001, p 47). Since there was a shortage of labour in many sectors of the economy, state enterprises provided training and employment for young people, and supported students in vocational training and at universities with grants as well as guaranteeing employment on graduation (p 51).

Welfare provisions were of a similar type across the Eastern Bloc countries (Deacon, 2000, p 147),

> [...] it consisted of the provision of highly subsidised prices on food, housing, transport, and basic necessities, guaranteed employment, adequate health and education provision and small differentials between the wages of workers, professionals and managers, in return for the political quietude of the population.

The shortcomings of this system included hidden privileges for state and party bureaucrats, and many of the benefits were insufficient or distributed unequally in favour of the nomenclature.

Women's emancipation was part of communist ideology (Molyneux, 1991).[11] Because of growth in the industrial sector in the communist countries and shortage of labour, women were an important part of the workforce. They worked alongside men in the same type of occupations, although with lower wages and less opportunities for promotion. In 1980 women comprised half the workforce in Eastern Europe (Molyneux, 1991, p 91), and in 1989 70-90 per cent of women aged 15-55 were in employment in the communist countries (Pollert, 2003, p 333). There was no part-time employment. However, women were also the main carers in families; indeed, Deacon (2000, p 147) describes the division of labour as 'sexist'. Women's 'double burden' was recognised by communist ideology and was to be remedied by paid maternity leave and childcare facilities (Molyneux, 1991). And as Pollert (2003, p 334) observes, universal healthcare contributed to women's wellbeing.

As noted above, the system of education in Communist countries was structured to meet the demands in the planned economy. Women gained access to professions that in the West were, and remain, male-dominated (Molyneux, 1991; Kovacheva, 2001; Pollert, 2003). In the mid-1980s one third of Soviet engineers were women (Molyneux, 1991). Because of the male dominance in occupations that led to promotion in the industrial sector, women's route upwards was through the education system (Pollert, 2003).

Broadly speaking, these were the conditions in the societies into which the interviewees in the Eastern European countries were born. During their childhood and early youth these conditions set the structural parameters for their life course, and their parents had lived their whole life within these social, political and economic circumstances. As will be discussed in succeeding chapters, the shift that the fall of communism created affected their adult lives in profound ways during the transition to parenthood.

South and west of the Iron Curtain

Non-democratic political regimes were also present in the West. Portugal was ruled by a dictatorship for 42 years until the 'Carnation Revolution' of April 1974 (Machado and da Costa, 2000). The nature of non-democracy did, however, vary considerably between Portugal (and indeed also the non-democratic regimes of Spain and Greece) and the Eastern European countries. Where the Portuguese regime made few efforts to improve the population's level of education or to reduce social inequality and widespread poverty (Machado and da Costa, 2000), the communist bloc countries raised educational standards and provided healthcare.

In all the Western countries there was structural change in the economy during the postwar period with a decline in the primary sector[12] (farming and fisheries), the start of a decline in the secondary (manufacturing) sector and an increase of employment in the service, or tertiary, sector. These changes went hand in hand with increasing urbanisation (Hobsbawm, 1994).

In this period more democratic access to education became available in Western countries. The education level of the populations increased and the number of the world's universities more than doubled in the 1970s (Hobsbawm, 1994, p 297). Of the European countries, Norway and Sweden had the largest expansions of upper secondary and university-level education (Stafseng, 1996). In Portugal the legacy of long years of dictatorship left the country with an illiteracy rate of 25.6 per cent in 1970, which decreased to 11 per cent in 1991 (Machado and da Costa, 2000, p 23). The expansion of its education system after the 'Carnation Revolution' in 1974 was formidable (Machado and da Costa, 2000, p 23), although the illiteracy rate remained high into the 1990s (Sebastião, 2000).

The Women's Movement started in Northern European countries in the 1970s. Second-wave feminists fought for free abortion,[13] equal rights to education and work, paid maternity leave, equal pay and public childcare (Holter, 1984). Ideas about gender equity that took root during the youth of our informants' parents remain ideals for many today rather than part of established practice. As the following chapters demonstrate, there is also variation between countries in the extent to which these ideas permeated policies and practice.

The expanding welfare states in Northern Europe in general, and in the Scandinavian countries such as Norway and Sweden in particular, was related to an extension of social security for the population, included study loans and free access to higher education, and also involved an increase in the public sector of the economy and consequently a higher percentage of women in occupations that entailed caring and teaching.

After the fall of communism, 1990-2003[14]

The interviewees in our study were born in an historical period (1965-75) that, as the previous sections have demonstrated, involved many changes that affected their life course in various ways. The differences between their own experiences and that of their parents produced intergenerational family change related to historical and period-specific changes that were taking place in the postwar period (Brannen et al, 2004).

Notably for the Portuguese interviewees, education was a new experience for many families as most parents and grandparents had not had access to secondary or higher education, with many illiterate. Portuguese sociologists have described the modernisation process as still ongoing, with the majority of the population living in the countryside until well into the 1980s (Machado and da Costa, 2000). The percentage of women in the workforce has increased steadily from 13.1 per cent in 1960 to 42.2 per cent in 1996 (de Almeida et al, 2000), with Portugal having the highest rate of women in full-time employment in Europe at the time of the study (Fagnani et al, 2004).

Interviewees from Bulgaria (and to a lesser extent Slovenia) enjoyed access to higher education since their societies' plan economy pursued full employment for both men and women. Until the fall of the Berlin wall and the downfall of the Soviet Union, most had upper secondary or higher education. The 1990s saw a dramatic shift in social, political and economic life in these countries (Kovacheva, 2001; Pollert, 2003). For Slovenia the shift also involved becoming an independent republic after the collapse of the former Yugoslavia together with subsequent wars and atrocities in the region. Slovenia is now a member of the EU, while Bulgaria at the time of the study was an applicant country.

In Northern European societies important changes affecting the interviewees' lives from the 1970s include the deregulation of capital and cuts in public spending affecting the regulation of employment and the provision of welfare. Housing policies also changed throughout most of Europe in this period. Where the postwar years had seen a political consensus across the spectrum in most West European countries, on Keynesian policies in general and on housing policies in particular, with public investments in house building being substantial, there was a change from the mid-1970s towards deregulation of capital and market economies when centre-right governments came into power in many countries (Balchin, 1996). Public investment in housing decreased and access to rented housing diminished,[15] particularly in the UK under the Thatcher government that took office in 1979.[16] In Sweden and the Netherlands the tendency towards privatisation and market 'solutions' to housing needs was not as pronounced as in other countries (Balchin, 1996). Access to affordable housing was an important issue in people's lives, and for the cohort interviewed in Transitions, the deregulation of housing markets across much of Europe created obstacles to establishing separate households from their families of origin.

As neoliberal economic and political ideas gradually took hold across all European countries, more flexible work arrangements were introduced (Lewis et al, 2009). Reduction in public spending also led to the outsourcing of jobs from the public sector to the private market, for example, cleaning, catering and clerical work. This change in the composition of the workforce in organisations, with employees on different types of contracts within the same organisation, was new (Kalleberg, 2000). A related novel trend was an increase in short-term work contracts (Kalleberg, 2000). Here there were variations between the countries, as laws governing the protection of labour remained strong in the Scandinavian countries and in Slovenia, whereas in the UK over the Thatcher era workers' protection and trades unions were weakened significantly. As the 'modernisation' of welfare states became a focus of political concern, the logic of New Public Management (NPM) and its cost-efficiency principles of for-profit businesses gained increasing influence in public sectors across Europe (Christensen and Lægreid, 2007).

These changes fuelled and were fuelled by globalisation, leading to a substantial reduction of employment in the secondary – or manufacturing – sector across Europe as companies exported manufacturing and service production to countries such as China and India, where labour costs were lower (Harvey, 2003).

A further general trend across Europe in the postwar period was the increase in women's labour market participation. This started in Northern European countries in the 1970s,[17] with the male breadwinner family being replaced by the two-income family as the standard in most households (Lewis, 2001), although many women adjusted their employment to working part time following the birth of children. This trend is only now beginning to be supported by public and employer support in some Northern European countries (Lewis et al, 2009). By contrast, Eastern European countries under communism provided full employment and public support (public childcare and paid leave) for working mothers (Pollert, 2003). However, while such support was in place at the time of the study, the arrival of private sector labour markets made it risky for parents to avail themselves of such support. Moreover, the gender division of labour in families remains persistently traditional across European countries (Knudsen and Waerness, 2008). Despite the changes in women's employment, all countries are characterised by gender-segregated labour markets, a point discussed more fully elsewhere (see Fagnani et al, 2004; Lewis et al, 2009).

Another major trend in the latter half of the 20th century was the start of a demographic shift caused by increased longevity in populations and falling fertility rates across most of Europe (Fagnani et al, 2004).[18]

Despite greater affluence in some countries and among some sectors of the population, many experience the current historical period as insecure (Sennett, 1998). As the nature of work is changing, the idea of 'jobs for life' that characterised postwar societies in Europe –East and West alike – is now being replaced by short-term work contracts and flexible employment patterns. As has been argued elsewhere on the basis of previous comparative research (Brannen et al, 2002), these new trends do not affect people's lives to the same extent or in the same way. In this book we map out how circumstances and contexts vary, and how these variations make for differences in both the patterning and experience of the transition to parenthood as it relates to other life course transitions and phases, across countries, organisational contexts, gender and social class.

In summing up briefly the contextual features that characterised the countries in the study in the period 1990-2003 in relation to their recent postwar history, we find it useful to make a distinction between a traditional North–South, East–West divide:

- *The Western European* countries in the study are urbanised societies with high levels of public sector employment, developed welfare state regimes, high levels of expenditure on healthcare and high education levels in the population. From the 1970s onwards these countries saw an increase in women's participation in the workforce, and the male breadwinner model was gradually replaced by the dual-income family, although among many families with young children the fathers continued to work full time with the mother working part time as in the UK, the Netherlands, Sweden and Norway.
- *The Southern European* country (Portugal) has a recent history of dictatorship, at the time of the study a low, although rapidly increasing, standard of living, a relatively high illiteracy rate (among some sectors of the population) and low expenditure on healthcare. Women's participation in the workforce increased after the fall of the dictatorship and the country's gradual modernisation process took hold. A high percentage of the population still live in rural areas, although migration to urban areas increased significantly over the post-revolution period. The two-income family is common and the percentage of women working full time the highest in Europe.
- *The Eastern European* countries (Bulgaria and Slovenia) are both former communist countries. There is a high level of education among adults. Following the transition to a market economy and a liberal political system the public sector is decreasing in size, with severe cuts in expenditure in health and education. There is a high percentage of women in the workforce, most working full time. The maternal leave period remains generous, and likewise public childcare still exists. Compared to Western Europe, a relatively high percentage of the population lives in rural communities.

Conclusion

This chapter has two distinct but interrelated parts. The first gave an overview of theoretical and conceptual features of a life course perspective which forms the overarching frame of analysis for the empirical evidence in the following chapters. The second part attempted to outline some broad trends over time at the institutional level within and across the countries involved in the Transitions study. Such a macro-historical overview is a necessary backcloth for understanding the layers of context in which to analyse the biographical material. As such it forms one of the several layers of context that together provide thick descriptions for the analysis of individual cases. In the next chapter we discuss the methodology of the study; such discussions highlight how biographical cases are well suited to the purpose of cross-national comparative research. We demonstrate in more detail how historical circumstances are essential for interpreting these in a contextualist life course perspective.

Notes

[1] For instance Jamieson, Callinicos, Harvey and Eagleton (Anderson, 1998, p 78).

[2] They adopt this term from Merton (1968, cited in Elder et al, 2006) and define it thus: 'Theoretical orientations establish a common field of inquiry by providing a framework for descriptive and explanatory research' (Elder et al, 2006, p 4).

[3] In disciplines such as criminology and particularly developmental psychology longitudinal studies had been common for most of the 20th century (Nilsen and Brannen, 2010).

[4] The contraceptive pill and other means by which to regulate reproduction are innovations that have had a huge impact on both women's and men's lives from the 1960s onwards.

[5] His classification is based on level of de-commodification that is defined as: 'the degree to which individuals and families can uphold a socially acceptable standard of living independently of market participation' (Esping-Andersen, 1990, p 37).

[6] Bonoli (1997) argues that Esping-Andersen's typology does not distinguish clearly enough between the Bismarckian and the Beveridgean approaches to social policy (p 357).

[7] Arts and Gelissen (2002) refer to the response from Esping-Andersen on the critique where he is inconsistent in, for instance, whether or not to include the countries of Southern Europe as a cluster of welfare regimes where families are the most important providers of welfare (pp 153-4).

[8] The average West European unemployment was 1.5 per cent in the mid-1960s (Hobsbawm, 1994, p 259).

[9] An important process that started in Western Europe in the 1950s was that of establishing economic collaboration across national borders. In April 1951, Germany, the Netherlands, France, Italy, Luxembourg and Belgium signed a treaty to run their heavy industries under one management. This was the first step towards what is today the European Union. In 1973 The UK and Denmark joined, and after the fall of communism many of the former Eastern Bloc countries also joined the EU. At the time of the study all participating countries except Norway and Bulgaria were members. Bulgaria was at the time an applicant country and has since become a full member. The EU has become a significant policy maker and maker of regulations that affect many areas of the financial and social spheres of life in the member countries and beyond, as Anderson (2009) observes, 'Yet in the life of the states that belong to it, politics – at an incomparably higher level of intensity – continues to be overwhelmingly internal' (p xi). A more detailed examination of the effects of EU membership on the trajectories of our interviewees is beyond the ambition and scope of this chapter. Suffice to state that Transitions was a cross-national study where individual countries formed the main macro context we examined.

[10] Although there were differences between the Bulgarian communist regime, with its tight collaboration with Moscow and the socialist regime in Yugoslavia under Tito, the two had more in common on a number of factors than they shared with the rest of Europe during the first part of the postwar era. However, there were fewer restrictions on the Yugoslavian population, for example, on travel, than those in existence in Bulgaria (Hobsbawm, 1994, p 396).

[11] Measures to emancipate women adopted by the 1920 Congress of the Comintern included: 'encouragement of women to work outside the home; the introduction of legal equality between men and women; the liberalisation of laws on the family and marriage; the promotion of equality of opportunity in education; and the prohibition of sexually exploitative images and writing, and of practices such as prostitution' (Molyneux, 1991, p 90).

[12] Hobsbawm (1994, p 289) says: 'The most dramatic and far-reaching social change of the second half of this century, and the one which cuts us off for ever from the world of the past, is the death of the peasantry'.

[13] This is still a controversial issue and access to abortion is restricted in most countries.

[14] Most interviews were conducted in 2003 and 2004.

[15] In Norway a conservative government came into power in 1981 and deregulated the housing market.

[16] In the UK one key area of change was in housing policy where investment in public housing decreased from the 1970s. The Thatcher government introduced the 'Right to Buy' to local authority tenants, resulting in a major sell off of public housing (Balchin, 1996).

[17] The Women's Movement coincided with the increase in women's labour force participation but cannot be seen as the reason for the increase. A number of factors pulled together to make the two-income family the new norm (Hobsbawm, 1994).

[18] This is a concern for political authorities across all countries and has, in many instances, led to measures to encourage families to have more children. Since the reasons for decisions for families' choice of number of children are many and complex, political measures to turn the demographic trend are rarely successful on their own.

THREE

Methodological approaches, practices and reflections

Julia Brannen and Ann Nilsen

Introduction

In the Transitions project we set out to examine how European men and women working in public and private sector workplaces negotiate motherhood and fatherhood and work–family boundaries in the context of different national welfare state regimes, family and employer support. We adopted a life course perspective, as described in Chapter Two. This enabled us to situate the transition to – and experience of – parenthood within the various structural and social domains in which individuals create their careers in work, education, and as partners and parents. It focused on seven countries in Eastern and Western Europe and on two types of work organisations: social services in the public sector and finance companies in the private sector (Nilsen and Brannen, 2005; Lewis and Smithson, 2006a).

The study has two main methodological features. First, it adopted a comparative qualitative approach. Second, it adopted an embedded case study design (Yin, 2003) in which working parents were studied with reference to three analytic levels: the macro level of national public policy provision; the organisational level of employer policies and provision and informal support in the workplace; and the individual level, the biographical trajectories of working parents. The contextualisation of individual lives facilitates the process of cross-national comparison and generates both differences and similarities within and across national settings.

The research design of Transitions requires a consideration of a number of methodological issues. In this book we address topics that relate to biographical methods and to comparative cross-national research. First, we examine some theoretical issues involved in cross-national, case-based research. Next, we set out the criteria used for the selection of cases of the parents in the study at the design stage and in the subsequent comparative analysis which form the basis of the subsequent chapters. Finally, we offer a few recommendations based on working with the approach.

Cross-national comparative case-based research

Comparative case-based research is a large field encompassing a number of perspectives, theories and methodological approaches.[1] Space does not permit an extensive overview of these, nor indeed is that our ambition here. We confine ourselves to a limited set of concerns that directly relate to the type of cross-national comparative research in which we have been involved.

Some argue that all social science research is *comparative* (Samuel, 1985), and there are different definitions of *cross-national* research (Kohn, 1987). Referring to the former, Hantrais suggests the following definition:

> ... [comparative research] is the term widely employed to describe studies of societies, countries, cultures, systems, institutions, social structures and change over time and space, when they are carried out with the intention of using the same research tools to compare systematically the manifestations of phenomena in more than one temporal or spatial socio–cultural setting. (Hantrais, 2009, p 15)

For others, comparative research is a distinct branch of research since 'it introduces time and space as controlling variables in generalisations concerned with the behaviour of social groups' (Samuel, 1985, p 7). At issue here is therefore not the method *per se* but rather the methodological approach that is adopted. So it would seem more appropriate to use the term 'comparative approaches' rather than 'comparative methods' (Hantrais, 2009).

Kohn (1987) makes a distinction between *implicit* and *explicit* cross-national comparative research, where the latter uses comparable data from two or more nations. He distinguishes between four types of explicit cross-national comparative research: 'those in which nation is *object* of study; those in which nation is a *context* of study; those in which nation is a *unit of analysis*; and those that are *transnational* in character' (Kohn, 1987, p 714).

In the analysis of the Transitions study, the national level was considered to be a context of study rather than 'the' unit of analysis or object of study. Kohn's definition of context of study refers to 'how certain social institutions operate or about how certain aspects of social structure impinge on personality' (p 714). In Transitions we were not concerned with issues of personality, but 'nation as context' is nevertheless a useful way of describing how an embedded case study approach takes cross-national characteristics into account. In this book 'country as context' is foregrounded depending on the chapters' foci; in some chapters other structural features form the criteria for comparison.

Case-based studies involve a *small* number of cases and interactions between *many* variables while statistical studies investigate a *large* number of cases and relatively *few* variables (Hammersley and Gomm, 2000). In other words, case-based studies rely on the production of what Geertz terms 'thick description', although Geertz' concept relates to a different methodological tradition than our own[2] (Geertz, 2000 [1973]). In practice Geertz' texts include more than one definition of thick description. As Hammersley (2008) observes, 'It is the set of questions being addressed [...] which provides the guide as to how thick a description should be, or rather where a description needs to be thick and where it does not' (p 67). In the Transitions study we use the term to apply to data collected through a variety of methods and to reflect different societal levels – national, organisational and individual. Further we situate the individual biographical cases in multiple layers of context thereby providing 'thick descriptions' of each case and of each case in relation to other cases.

In qualitative case study research, debate hinges on issues of 'generalisability', although many such researchers would eschew this term altogether (Hammersley, 2008). The term 'generalisation' originates in quantitative research that employs probability samples that are large enough to yield results that are representative of a population and are thus regarded as generalisable to larger populations. However, as Gobo (2008) observes, '[...] probability/representativeness and generalisability are not two sides of the same coin. The former is a property of the *sample*, whilst the latter concerns the *findings* of research' (p 194). As Gobo goes on to suggest, the range of different activities that occur between the construction of the sample and the confirmation of hypotheses often impairs the connection between the sample and the quality of the findings. Hence, a large sample with many cases is no guarantee of representative data, or of reliable generalisation.

Where generalisation is taken to mean assessing the relevance of the findings of case-based research beyond the particular case, a range of other terms have been used to describe this process. Stake (2000) uses the term '*naturalistic generalisation*' while Lincoln and Guba (1985) speak in terms of the *transferability* of findings in which the burden of proof is on the user rather than the researcher once the latter's job is done.[3]

Case comparisons engage in both generalisation and specification, as Mjøset (2007) observes, referring to comparative case study sociology of a macro kind. Generalisation can involve drawing theoretical inferences, that is, the extrapolation of the features of a case to a theoretically similar type of case or situation, or it can involve empirical generalisation, for example, generalisation to a larger number of cases. The former is associated with experimental research and the latter with surveys (Gomm et al, 2000, p 102). Both types may also apply to case studies: '[…] it is possible for case study work to have general relevance without empirical generalisation across cases, through reliance on theoretical inference' (Gomm et al, 2000, p 103). However, a great deal of data about the cases and the population they are drawn from is needed to demonstrate their typicality. As noted above, the Transitions study collected different types of data and covered different contexts. While it is not possible to present all these data here, they inform the analysis of the biographical material.

Case selection

If cases are selected from a homogeneous population, it is easier to generalise empirically and theoretically. Gomm et al (2000) recommend *systematic* sampling of cases in order to enhance their generalisability, while recognising that selection is often a matter of pragmatics. Transparency and rigour in the selection of cases are crucial. From a theoretical perspective, cases must be 'cases of something' (Hammersley and Gomm, 2000). In Transitions cases were selected purposively by applying a sociological rather than a statistical logic (Gobo, 2008). However, case selection occurs at several phases in the research. In the design phase the framework for case selection at all levels is decided. At the fieldwork stage practical and other circumstances may lead to changes where 'second best' alternatives have to be chosen without altering the overall design. In the phase of analysis sub-selections of cases may be decided depending on purpose. However, at all these levels notions of typicality arise. Schofield (2000) argues that:

> Selection on the basis of typicality provides the potential for a good "fit" with many other situations. Thick description provides the information necessary to make informed judgements about the degree and extent of that fit in particular cases of interest. (p 78)

Knowledge about the wider context from which the cases are chosen is necessary both for selection and analysis purposes (Gomm et al, 2000). In Transitions the first phases of the study focused on extensive context mapping in all countries (Fagnani et al, 2004) and overviews of relevant literature in each country (den Dulk et al, 2003). Each national team that took part in the study included experienced researchers in their fields, several of whom had collaborated in earlier cross-national studies (Brannen et al, 2002). Each team therefore brought a wealth of international and national knowledge of both primary and secondary research evidence to the study that further strengthened thick descriptions and contextualisation.

Concerning the *choice of countries*, the project sought to include a spatial distribution that was within the boundaries of the EU's funding prerequisites at the time. Within these limitations the countries were selected according to type of welfare regime: two Nordic countries with egalitarian welfare states (Sweden and Norway); two liberal welfare states (the UK and the Netherlands), in addition to Portugal that has a more familialistic welfare system, and Bulgaria and Slovenia (Eastern Europe) whose welfare states do not fall into categories described by Esping-Andersen (1990). However, this latter classification was not considered sufficient background for the study's purposes given that a life course approach, which was part of the overarching research design, involves taking a broader set of institutional frameworks into consideration (Elder et al, 2006; Blossfeld, 2009) in order to provide thick descriptions of 'countries as contexts'.

The *organisations* were selected on the basis of principles of similarity and difference. We sought organisations from the private and the public sector in each country since type of sector affects employees' experiences: social services in the 'human services' public sector and finance organisations in the 'for profit' private sector. In most countries wages were higher in the private than the public sector; on the whole jobs were more secure in the public sector; more women were employed in public sector occupations and so on (Crompton et al, 2003; Tronstad, 2007). Up to 10 managers from different levels of each organisation were interviewed and documentary information was collected about the organisations. Mothers and fathers with a youngest child under 12 years old took part in workplace-based focus groups (between 4 and 11 focus groups per organisation). From these we recruited participants for the biographical interviews.

In the selection of *biographical cases* we aimed to conduct at least 10 interviews with parents from each workplace. We sought to compare cases of working mothers and fathers born between 1965 and 1975 who had children under 12 and similar occupational statuses within similar organisations (see Box 3.1). We also sought to include some lone mothers in each sector (one high status and one low status), but this proved difficult in some cases. All these criteria set the boundaries for what our interviewees are 'cases of'.

Box 3.1: Selection categories for interviews

Cases selected for each private and public sector organisation (11 for each organisation)

4 partnered mothers in high-status occupations (professional or managerial)
1 lone mother in a high-status occupation
2 partnered mothers in low-status occupations (clerical or manual)
1 low-status single mother in a low-status occupation
2 fathers, one high status and one low status
1 agency worker (mother or father), a skilled or semi-skilled worker

---

There were many practical limits to achieving comparability. Countries form the wider context for comparisons (Kohn, 1987), and EU guidance on the appropriate mix of countries described above constrained our range of choices here. At the organisational level we encountered a number of obstacles.[4] In the private sector it was difficult to find comparable organisations in one particular type of business; teams adopted different solutions with some countries gaining access to banks, others insurance and in one case a private sector multinational company. Not all national teams had the funding to carry out organisational case studies in both sectors; both sectors were studied in four countries (UK, Norway, Portugal and Bulgaria) and one sector only was studied in three countries (the finance sector in Slovenia and the Netherlands, and the public sector in Sweden). However, this presented ample opportunity for both cross-sector and same sector comparisons.

At the biographical level, there were constraints on comparability. Although we sought to include a majority of partnered interviewees, we also aimed to include some currently single parents. In some countries we found no lone parents in the relevant groups, while in other instances we found former lone parents who were in new partnerships. Moreover, one employee who was a lone parent when he took part in the workplace focus group had a new partner by the time of the biographical interview, thus demonstrating that lone parenthood is best conceptualised as a life course phase. In some contexts, we found few parents in manual low-skilled jobs since many such jobs had been outsourced. We also found large variations in educational levels required for apparently similar types of jobs. For example, the qualifications demanded for social work differed between countries, with high educational levels among social workers in Sweden and Norway that were achieved earlier in the life course (Nilsen et al, 2009; Plantin and Bäck-Wiklund, 2009) compared with that attained among social workers in the UK and Portugal (Brannen, 2009; das Dores Guerreiro et al, 2009). Indeed, taking the whole populations, educational levels are higher in the two Scandinavian countries compared with Portugal and the UK (OECD, 2008).

Selecting cases for analysis in the book

In the book, cases were chosen for comparison depending on the foci of the chapters. Moreover, cases were chosen on the basis of the principles of similarity or difference. When choosing cases for discussion in Chapters Four and Five concerning parents' life course and their trajectories into parenthood, we foregrounded the national level, making it the main axis for the initial comparison. The rationale behind country selection in the Transitions project has been discussed above. In Chapters Four and Five we chose cases from different countries in the three categories outlined in Chapter Two, that is, Northern, Southern and Eastern Europe. National context is formative in shaping the institutional systems of education, welfare and the labour market and thereby shape the opportunities available to individuals, although they also interact with other structural features to do with gender, social class and ethnicity. Comparing cases across such contexts therefore gives insight into the influence of structure on individual agency in the forming of trajectories that a one-country study could not provide.

When we turned to another dimension of analysis, the current experience of being working parents and the resources they deploy to support them and their children (Chapter Seven), a different dimension for comparison was selected and came into play. Here it was considered important to compare parents within *similar occupations* and work contexts to see how their occupation and work contexts had an impact on them in specific national and organisational contexts together with the importance of a range of other resources: parental leave schemes, childcare provided nationally or by local communities and forms of informal support. As we will show within a particular sector and among workers in similar occupations living in different countries, it is the convergence of the available or unavailable resources that is critical for the experience of working parenthood. The patterns of available or unavailable resources do, however, vary between countries, demonstrating how a cross-national approach is relevant even if other factors are more influential in shaping a person's opportunities in a particular context at a particular time.

Biographical interviews

As set out in Chapter Two, a life course perspective (Elder et al, 2006) informed the design of the Transitions study in general, and the choice of biographical methods for the individual interviews. A biography can be defined as a *story told in the present* about a person's *life in the past* and his or her *expectations for the future* (Kohli, 1981). Three elements are important in a biography: the factual events in the person's life; the meaning these have for the person; and the way the story about the person is told. All must be interpreted with reference to the different layers of context within which a life unfolds.

Our experiences with biographical interviewing and other qualitative in-depth interviews suggested a design that took the temporal aspects of narrative into account (Brannen and Nilsen, 2002a, 2002b, 2005; Nilsen, 1994, 1996). The interview guide was thus designed to capture different temporal dimensions but also to tackle these in particular ways and to direct the interviewee to particular time frames rather than giving the interviewee the freedom to cover their whole life story in an unstructured way, as is often the practice with other biographical methods (Wengraf, 2001). Moreover, this was considered appropriate, as not all members of the cross-national team were experienced in biographical methods.

One way to start a biographical interview is to focus on the present. In the interview guide we suggested to the research teams that the interviewer begin with an open question. The question most teams started with was, 'Could you tell me a little bit about yourself and your life?'. In many instances, this led the informant into a summary narrative of his or her life. A line of questioning was then recommended to open up the *present* and enable a focus on 'current concerns', with the interviewer choosing which themes to proceed with, either family or work, since these were the twin foci of the study. The present was followed by a focus on the *past*. The informant was asked to think back to when he or she was aged 20. In reminding the interviewee of the actual age, the interviewer jogged the interviewee's memory by bringing back key events relating to the particular year. The same specific temporal instruction was given to the future – informants were asked to think about their work and family lives 10 years from the interview. In the last part of the interview we returned to the present and explored strategies and practices relating to the ways in which they negotiated the domestic division of labour and childcare in their families with their partners and how far they sought to and were able to keep separate their working lives from their family lives.

Given that not all the cross-national team was equally experienced in biographical interviewing, we ensured time for training in the method at a project meeting. Test biographical interviews between team members were conducted at one of our international team meetings. This proved very valuable and team members found the method interesting and the exercise a learning experience.

Lifeline analysis

The life course perspective requires the researcher to take into account the timing of age-related and other transitions and life course phases. Following each biographical interview a 'lifeline' was plotted for each individual parent, in order to depict graphically the timing, sequencing and length of the key phases and events in the life course, as we show in Chapters Four and Five. Earlier studies suggest they are helpful in cross-national comparison (see, for example, Bjerén and Elgqvist-Saltzman, 1994; Nilsen, 1994). We also found this a particularly useful strategy since it enabled the international team individually and collectively to contextualise the individual cases within their societal contexts. In our international team meetings, we examined the lifelines as a group identifying the sectoral or country-specific features which were relevant to the particular working parents whom we interviewed. The lifelines proved useful in identifying patterns of linearity and nonlinearity in education and employment trajectories and differences by gender and social class, and also in understanding the timing of the transition to parenthood in interviewees' lives. They helped the team to compare individuals within countries as well as between countries. Thus they demonstrate graphically different trajectories into parenthood: those where there was a confluence of other transitions around the transition to parenthood, notably the start of a relationship, finding housing and childbirth happening around the same time; and those where the pattern was more staggered and normative for the period, namely where life course transitions were spaced out forming a linear pattern over a longer time period.

Comparative case analysis of the biographical cases

Biographical case analysis can provide a nuanced picture of transition patterns and highlight agency by focusing on the accounts people give for the direction of their lives. A key aspect of comparing the biographical cases concerned participants' trajectories into education and work and how these influenced the timing and experience of the transition to parenthood and other social transitions (Chapters Four and Five). The analysis and presentation of cases shows how, in the detail of the case, a trajectory is forged and made sense of by the person and the way in which different institutional contexts shape parents' life course trajectories, mediated by class, ethnicity and gender.

For the initial phase of analysis frameworks in relation to the main questions posed in the interviews were developed for common use by all the national teams, reflecting the research questions in Transitions. In this phase some teams sought to replicate similar analyses done by other teams in the course of analysing their own case study data. Given the biographical method that we adopted, analysing the data was also more difficult for some teams than for others. Summaries for each of the individual parent interviews were written according to a number of specified headings together with the opportunity to note themes that were abstracted inductively from the cases. Each parent summary was then translated into English and exchanged between teams. The idea was for each team to seek elucidation of any taken-for-granted contextual and cultural issues that were not spelt out in the summaries. In the same way drafts of the national reports on the interview phase of the study (and other national reports) were exchanged between the teams and discussed in groups.

Language is of particular importance in cross-national comparative analysis. Few projects have enough funding to make translation of all interviews feasible, and this was case in this study. As already noted, teams were asked to provide summaries of each interview in English. The depth and length of these summaries varied greatly between countries, again relating to fluency in written English but also raising questions about the depth and quality of the original data, although this was not possible to assess. In writing up the report of this phase of the study (the consolidated interview report), the authors were reliant on the analysis provided in the parent summaries and the national interview reports. In comparative qualitative analysis, this is less than satisfactory. Access to interviews in full is a much better way to facilitate comprehensive cross-national comparative analysis. However, there are ways around this, as our efforts have shown. In particular, the occasions for teams to feed back their interpretation of other teams' cases sometimes confirmed the original interpretation or suggested fresh interpretations. More commonly they generated gaps in the data or omissions from the analysis that the analyst needed to flesh out further. For example, the gap could reflect the interviewer's failure to ask a particular question or the analyst's failure to point to the particular features of a respondent's situation and context. It might indicate that a parent did not perceive a particular feature of their situation as supportive, for example, when this was clearly relevant to their situation. In writing the chapters for this book, co-authors include team members from countries where cases originate, thus giving access to the full interview material for the analysis of each topic covered.

It is of course true that biographical interviews capture what is unique for the individual. At one level therefore, the cases only represent themselves. However, as Bertaux (1990) observes, the analyst needs to find the 'right persons' to study, ask relevant questions and identify 'the implicit sets of rules and norms, the underlying situations, processes and contradictions that have both made actions and interactions possible and that have shaped them in specific ways' (pp 167-8). In this study, finding the 'right persons' involved the selection of informants whose lives related to or fitted with the study's specific research questions concerning the transition to parenthood and being a working parent. In the analysis of the interviews, understanding of the wider context was necessary, which put a considerable onus on the expertise and training of the researchers. As Bertaux observes, 'It takes some training to hear, behind the solo of a human voice, the music of society and culture in the background' (1990, pp 167-8).

Conclusion

In this chapter we have considered the methodological aspects of a particular type of cross-national research, namely case study research that employs qualitative methods and that addresses different layers of context. Such a design and mode of analysis can make visible what may be glossed over or be less evident when only one layer of context is taken into account, as in the case of a cross-national survey. A study that relies only on one layer of context, for example, the macro level of public policy support, misses important nuances concerning variations in individual experience, the meaning that people give to their lives and how their agency is shaped in and by different layers of context.

In the book, as we shall demonstrate in the following chapters, we tease out for certain people the particular conditions that shaped their lives in the transition to parenthood, for example, the age-related expectations within a particular society that govern social transitions as these are shaped by educational opportunities and related employment opportunities and so on. In the next section (we identify the structural features against which people managed as working parents and the resources they drew on at a particular life course phase of being a working parent with a young child: public policies and employer practices, housing provision and the help and support provided informally by kin and by others. We show how these intersected and affected parents' lives. However, it is important to note that only some relevant contextual features of individuals' situations emerged *explicitly* in informants' interviews. In cases where these were not mentioned specifically by interviewees, we still had to look out for them in the analysis (see Brannen and Nilsen, 2002, 2005). This is a benefit of a cross-national life course approach and of a design that seeks to capture different tiers of context. For example, parents did not always refer to public policy support or to the impact of their public/private sector employment conditions. But since the study covered these issues in other phases of the research, we were able to bring these to bear in the individual case analysis.

Comparing individual lives in the round is complex and comparing lives in different national contexts even more so. A combination of a life course perspective and a biographical method provided insight into both structure and agency. However, this also adds to the complexity of the design of a cross-national study. Comparative case-based research has its strengths and weaknesses. It can provide rich descriptions of a *few cases* which can make it possible to extrapolate from single cases knowledge that is transferable to other cases under similar conditions (Lincoln and Guba, 1985) and it can contribute to theoretical insights (Gomm et al, 2000). This design also has weaknesses – it can be costly and time consuming, and it requires highly experienced research teams that can apply similar procedures and adhere to the same standards. It requires developing the art of writing – case studies require a consistent and systematic approach and an ability to manage large amounts of untidy and unwieldy qualititative material that is often not neatly comparative. Writing up such material is a skill that has to be learned like other research skills.

Case studies are open to the charge of lack of rigour and lack of typicality (Schofield, 2000). However, an important criterion of rigour lies in case selection (Gomm et al 2000). In the overview of the research design and research process of Transitions, we sought to show how in all aspects of its design case selection was based on a sociological rather than a statistical logic (Gobo, 2008). Qualitative case study research also makes clear how important and difficult it is to achieve comparability, an issue that survey research tends to paper over through the process of statistical controls. Case-based studies can show the common and unique features of lives across time and space. They do this through thick descriptions and a rigorous analysis of relatively few cases set in multiple layers of context. They thereby shed insight into differences between seemingly similar cases and similarities between different cases. Such analyses may also demonstrate how particular lives could be led were social conditions changed and resources differently distributed.

In analysing comparative material of a qualitative nature we end with a few recommendations. The researcher wishing to embark on case-based comparative research in an international context may wish to take account of the following:

- Carry out modest amounts of comparative qualitative data analysis, at least in the first instance.
- Recognise that comparative cross-national work involves a dialogue between teams and provide time for this in the timetable.
- Realise it takes time, and a lot of invisible work, to build successful cross-national teams and to carry out comparative qualitative analysis; build this into the planning stages of projects.
- Spell out – don't iron out – conflicting or unclear interpretations of the material.
- Draw on contextual material where there are gaps or silences in the data.
- Take account of and discuss different methodological and theoretical traditions of the team members.
- Have policies in place relating to data ownership, authorship, archiving and English language domination.
- If methods are employed which are new to some team members run a methods training workshop, and involve external experts in this.
- Be prepared for the fact that some of the most productive writing often occurs after the project has ended.

Notes

[1] For a comprehensive discussion of comparative approaches see Mjøset (2007).

[2] Geertz (2000 [1973]) used the term now widely adopted in social science in cultural anthropology; he adapted it from Ryle (1971, cited in Gomm et al, 2000, p 101) contrasting it with 'thin descriptions' (Geertz, 2000 [1973]).

[3] Lincoln and Guba (1985), working within social constructivism, dismiss the concept and practice on positivist grounds. Transferability, used in a contextual approach, has merits in demonstrating the relevance of case studies.

[4] Although all countries had social services of some kind, they were organised differently.

FOUR

Comparing transitions to motherhood across contexts

Ann Nilsen, Maria das Dores Guerreiro, Siyka Kovacheva and Janet Smithson

Introduction

As the average age of the birth of the first child has increased significantly for women in most European countries, and the transition period between youth and adulthood for many has been prolonged, the transition to motherhood must be seen in relation to other life course trajectories and discussed with reference to social class and educational level, as well as institutional arrangements such as welfare provision, workplace regulations and systems of education in national contexts. This chapter therefore examines and compares different types of trajectories and transitions to motherhood. It takes a biographical case approach and analyses selected cases of mothers from four of the seven countries in the study. In order to give 'thick descriptions' (Geertz 2000 [1973]) of individual cases many layers of empirical context are brought to bear on the analysis.

Transition to motherhood in context

Women's average age at birth of the first child varied between the seven countries. Figures from 1999 show that Bulgaria has the lowest age, at approximately 25 years, whereas the Netherlands and Sweden have an average age at nearly 30 (Fagnani et al, 2004, pp 113-14). The tendency for European women to become mothers relatively late in the life course compared to a few decades ago must be seen in relation to the extended period of education that has become common in most countries. There are still persistent class divisions with respect to length and level of higher education: middle-class young people have more education than young people of working-class background. Women with little or no higher education tend to become mothers earlier in the life course. This is a trend across all countries (Fagnani et al, 2004, pp 113-14).

The transition to motherhood typically follows a period of cohabitation and/or marriage and finding a house or a flat in which to 'settle down' and establish a family.[1] In some countries, particularly in Southern and Eastern Europe, marriage and parenthood often happen while living in the parental home before the young couple is able to move to independent housing (Kovacheva, 2000; Roberts, 2009).

In this chapter we have chosen to focus on cases from four countries only. These are selected with reference to the discussion of historical context in Chapter Two. The layers of context in which individual lives unfold need to be understood within a comparative macro-level framework. The four countries cover the main dividing lines outlined in Chapter Two: the former Eastern bloc is represented by Bulgaria, a Scandinavian social democratic system represented by Norway, a neoliberal government by the UK and a new Southern European democracy by Portugal. Discussion of and comparisons in the transition to motherhood follow the framework provided by a life course perspective, thus the timing and scheduling of motherhood in relation to other life course phases and transitions is described first. Workplace differences in terms of private or public sector employment have been discussed elsewhere (Lewis et al, 2009) and will not be the focus of the following discussion.

Becoming a mother in a post-communist country in transition: Bulgaria

Bulgaria has the lowest average age of first-time births for women of the countries in the study. But here as elsewhere there is an overall tendency for young people to postpone parenthood until later in the life course. The timing of motherhood is related to the timing of other life course phases and transitions, notably higher education and labour market entry. As discussed earlier, social class differences are related to the timing of labour market entry: those who have no higher education tend to enter the labour market earlier and also to have children earlier in the life course.

Cases from Bulgaria illustrate this point. While the average age for birth of the first child has risen since the fall of communism,[2] young people with higher education tend to postpone parenthood compared to those with manual low-paid jobs requiring no higher qualifications. It is not uncommon for Bulgarian young people to live with parents and in-laws after establishing their own families. This is due to the difficult housing situation. Only half of the 23 parents in the Bulgarian study lived in independent households. Obtaining independent housing for young families is 'a family project in which not only the resources of the couple but also the resources of the extended family were mobilised' (Kovacheva and Matev, 2005, p 23).

The Bulgarian study identified contextualised main patterns of the transition to adulthood and to motherhood in relation to social class: *direct transitions* involve short, linear trajectories from school to work, followed by early marriage and children, keeping the same job and expecting the future to be a continuation of the present. This pattern is associated with lower qualifications and lower job levels, and has similarities to the category 'early adulthood' described in Chapter One. *Prolonged transitions* involve many years of higher education followed by a period of temporary work that eventually leads to a permanent work contract, then marriage and children. This non-linear pattern is more frequent among the higher-educated and higher-status employees and bears some resemblance to the 'young adults' mentioned earlier.

Figure 4.1: Rosa

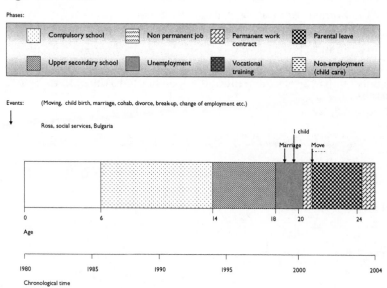

Rosa (24) represents the first trajectory – a direct linear pattern of transition. Born in 1980 to a working-class family, she left school at 18 without university entrance exams and held odd jobs for a year and then became pregnant with her future husband at 19. When she found out that she was pregnant, she had to make many choices simultaneously:

'I wasn't even 20 when I got pregnant. The flat wasn't ready yet and I didn't have a job. We had to sort out everything in one year before the baby came.'

For the first few months the couple lived with her parents. After getting married a few months later they moved into their own flat where they were still living at the time of the interview.

Within a year Rosa had a husband, a baby and a job in the lower ranks of social services. The job was necessary in order to receive maternity leave pay and other parental benefits provided by the state. She had a permanent job contract at the time of the interview and had worked for the municipality for five years by then, three of which had been on maternity leave. Her experience of the transition to parenthood is one of help and assistance from her mother and mother-in-law, and support from the wider family. Her main ambition in life was to have a family of her own. She was happy with the way things had worked out and hoped that the future would follow the current pattern in her life. Her job was not seen in terms of a 'career', but simply as a way of earning a living. Rosa's is typical of the old pattern of working-class life for women (Kovacheva et al, 2004), and of a transition from youth to adulthood within the category of 'early adulthood'.

In contrast to Rosa is **Nelly**, a 28-year-old social worker with higher education and a two-year-old child. She comes from a working-class family but had a very different outlook on life and a different trajectory

Figure 4.2: Nelly

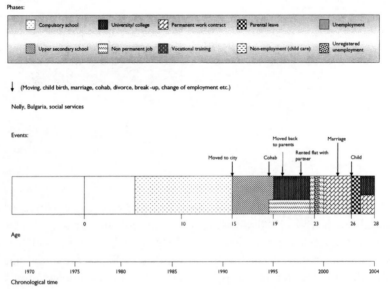

from that of Rosa. Her parents lived in a village. At 15 Nelly moved to a bedsit in a city in order to attend upper secondary school. She combined full-time studies with part-time employment to augment the support provided by her parents. The decision to go to university on finishing her upper secondary education she saw as 'an impulse':

> 'My choice was absolutely random – an impulse. There was no one in 1994 who knew what this specialisation – social pedagogy – was about. Afterwards it turned out that it was something that suited my personality, my understanding of the world, my needs. It was fate I think.'

When she got her degree she did not have any clear plans and found work as a waitress for a year without a work contract. She had to earn a living and since she lacked the network connections needed to find work in the field she was qualified for, she opted for a different occupation as a temporary solution. The traditional route to the higher echelons of occupational hierarchies is typically through social networks (family or friends) in influential positions. A non-governmental organisation (NGO) provided an opening for her and she got work to train as a child protection officer with this organisation that was later taken over by the state and was turned into a child protection unit. She was given a permanent work contract with this unit and only then did she marry her long-term cohabitee who was employed in a working-class occupation. At 26 she became pregnant.

> 'I felt that I am ready, that if it comes I will cope with it, but it wasn't specially planned, it was not an aim.... I always thought life was a very big responsibility. I was prepared to take care of myself, to earn enough money for myself. But taking care of a child was something I always thought was even more difficult and demanding, even more responsibility.'

Nelly demonstrates a career-oriented view to her work, and did not see herself as a full-time mother. She went back to work when her daughter was four months old, full time. The crèches in Bulgaria do not accept children under eight months old so childcare became an issue. In the end she had to take what is described as the typical Bulgarian childcare decision and involve her mother. The baby stayed with grandparents until she was old enough to go to a nursery. Her husband was away a lot and Nelly's work was very demanding with long hours. She experienced this phase as very busy and tiring. Her husband changed his work schedule to be able to take more of a part in the everyday care of their child and the situation improved for the whole family.

Nelly's transition to parenthood and her life course trajectory in general represents a new pattern in Bulgarian society. She was married to a man with lower qualifications and career prospects than her own, a pattern that was previously very unusual but has now become more common. Among social workers she belonged to a new group of employees who saw their jobs in terms of careers with promotion opportunities and self-development potential.[3] The Bulgarian examples illustrate mothers' high dependence on the extended family. Embedded in complex webs of relationships that provide support of various types, these young mothers' stories demonstrate how the different layers of context are important for understanding the biographical accounts about this phase in their lives. The shift from state-owned capital and generous state support to privatisation and cuts in state services have underlined the importance of the wider family network for the current generation of young parents.

Becoming a mother in a social democratic country: Norway

A different national context illustrates other varieties of trajectories in the transition to motherhood. The Scandinavian countries have egalitarian welfare state regimes and also student loans and grants that provide easier access to higher education than in many of the other countries in the study. There are also comparatively generous benefits for young parents in terms of parental leave. The average age at birth of the first child is just below 30 in Norway and Sweden, with considerable social class differences. As in Bulgaria, those of working-class background and occupations have children earlier in life than those who have higher education and higher-status occupations (Ellingsæter et al, 1997; Lappegård, 1999).

Although the Scandinavian countries score high on the GEM and GDI indexes,[4] Norway has one of the most gender-segregated labour markets in Europe (Ellingsæter and Solheim, 2002). Women on average do more housework than their male partners, and the part-time employment rate is high. The cohorts to which the Norwegian interviewees belong are highly educated. Approximately 80 per cent completed upper secondary school and a high percentage went on to higher education (Fagnani et al, 2004).

For Norwegians life course trajectories are highly related to type of upper secondary education and whether or not university entrance qualifications are obtained at the age of 19. In these cases a distinction was made between linear and non-linear trajectories, with a semi-linear type constituting a third pattern. These types must be understood in their historical context. An 'atypical' pattern for today's women might be 'typical' for the Norwegian housewife generation 40 years ago.[5] One of the interviewees presented below has a trajectory similar to the older generation, and is very atypical of the majority of the cohort she belongs to, but more typical of young women with little education. The lifelines and biographies must therefore also be interpreted with social class in mind.

The linear lifelines show how an informant moves from one life course phase to the next without any gaps or disruptions between them. The transition from upper secondary to higher education, and then from studying to waged work and on to cohabitation/marriage to childbirth is linear. However, a trajectory that does not involve higher education may also be linear if it involves a move from education to continuous employment, what in the Bulgarian cases was named a direct transition. Gendered aspects of linearity can also involve periods of non-employment and/or reduced working hours for mothers in relation to childbirth. This does not, however, necessarily make for a non-linear trajectory, only a female form of linearity that, because of its gaps, makes it different from a male linear model. Non-linear patterns on the other hand are associated with atypical timings of transitions in the life course compared to the trajectories of peers. Having a child early in life can involve non-linearity in employment trajectories depending on the circumstances, as the cases below demonstrate. Non-linearity can also be associated with the timing of education in the life course. Quite a few of the social workers went to college rather late in life after having held other jobs. This is a form of non-linearity where early choices in the life course are not 'irreversible'; they can be remedied without very high cost, that is, if earlier upper secondary qualifications that are necessary for university entrance are obtained. Those dropping out of school without such qualifications would have a harder time getting back into education since it would involve finding income other than from waged work for a longer period of time. As one of the cases below demonstrates, few were able to do this.

Gro is a rather extreme example of an extended linear trajectory in a Norwegian context. She is a 36-year-old engineer working for a private sector company, comes from a middle-class background and is married to her long-term cohabitee and has a one-year-old child. Her education trajectory is linear but extended. At 19, after upper secondary she moved out of her parents' home and went straight to university to do a Master's degree in engineering. The year she graduated she met her partner and started working for a multinational. She got a permanent work contract and has been in the same job since. Gro is atypical in that she graduated from a male-dominated education and is employed in a male-dominated profession. Her wage level is very high, and she enjoys a lifestyle that is dependent on high earnings. She is very committed to her work and took only eight months parental leave out of the 10 months with full pay to which she was entitled. Her partner took extended parental leave, four months in contrast to the one-month daddy leave parental leave to which he was entitled. Her trajectory takes the form of an extended linear pattern that reflects much more the lifelines of *men* in the multinational than those of her female colleagues regardless of job level. When talking about the decision to have a child she says:

> 'When you get to my age you have to make a choice ... you have to start thinking about it by the age of 35. It was unthinkable that I would never ever want one, had I been 25 I would probably have postponed it. It was actually my husband who brought it up and asked if we'd give it a think. And when I'd thought about it for a couple of months ... we decided.'

Figure 4.3: Gro

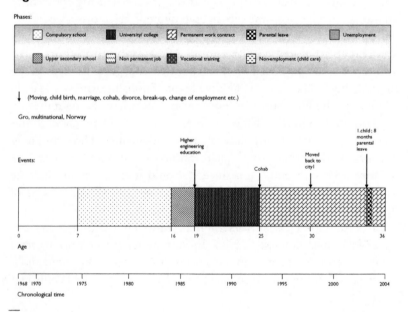

Her husband was a very committed father and Gro presented herself as a 'feminist' who demanded equal sharing of childcare and domestic work. In spite of it being unusual at her husband's workplace to take extended leave, he nevertheless was supported by his colleagues and managers in his decision to do this.

Gro is an example of an unusually smooth transition to parenthood, where everything was 'in place' before the child was born: a caring and committed partner, higher education completed, a well-paid, high-status occupation and a house of their own. Her life course pattern, although far from typical in any sense, is more frequently found among women from upper middle-class backgrounds. Her choice of education and occupation led her into a competitive male-dominated work environment and a job she clearly enjoyed. As with one of the UK cases presented below, Gro experienced a long transition phase from youth to adulthood, a group that in an earlier study was described as 'the young adults' (Nilsen et al, 2002; Brannen and Nilsen, 2005, this volume), those whose lives are affluent enough to involve *choice of lifestyle* and careful planning of parenthood in relation to life course phase and lifestyle preferences.

A contrasting case to that of Gro is **Jorunn**. She is 33 years old and works for a cleaning agency and was currently a contract worker at the multinational. She came from a working-class background and had no upper secondary education. She left school at 16 and met her future partner, got pregnant and had her first child at 17. Her partner provided for them for eight years while she was a housewife. The couple bought a flat in a high-rise block. Their second child was born when she was 22. When she was 25 her partner became ill and had to reduce his working hours. She started working for the agency part time since the family needed the income to get by. When her husband's condition got worse and he had to go on disability benefit, she started working full time as a cleaner. By then she was a contract worker at the multinational and has been there ever since. By the time she had her third child she had been in employment for long enough to claim paid maternity leave. She took a whole year off and went back to full-time work in the same job.

Asked about the decision to become a mother, Jorunn replied: 'I don't know... it just happened. And then we got two more....'

The timing of Jorunn's transition to parenthood and her lack of upper secondary education make for a direct transition to motherhood and non-linear work and education trajectories. It is more common for working-class women to have their first child earlier in life than for those of middle-class background. However, the fact that Jorunn did not have upper secondary education of any type, neither academic nor vocational, sets her apart. Her level of skills gave her few options occupation-wise in a country where the level of education for her cohort was very high. Most of her contemporaries had at least 12 years of schooling. The trajectory is characterised by her having made some choices early in life that could be seen as irreversible:

> 'I don't have an education and going back to school has never been an option, I couldn't bear the thought!'

Figure 4.4: Joruun

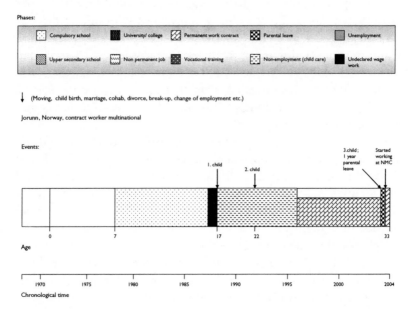

Jorunn, Norway, contract worker multinational

The family needed the money she earned as her husband was on a benefit scheme that provided a very low income. They lived near her family who provided some childcare and assistance with other practical tasks. For Jorunn this was of great importance and support over the years.

Jorunn's early transition to parenthood and her lack of higher education involve what we have elsewhere termed 'early adulthood' (Nilsen et al, 2002). This is characterised by having adult responsibilities, such as parenthood and/or having to support oneself through wage work, early in life. A very narrow opportunity structure because of lack of formal qualifications, and consequently fewer options to choose from both education and occupation-wise, make for a 'getting by mentality' in relation to life course transitions. Such difficult conditions hamper long-term planning (Nilsen et al, 2002, pp 173-5).

Another case that illustrates an early transition to motherhood is **Ingunn**, a 34-year-old engineer from the multinational. She came from an upper middle-class family and followed a linear path through the system of education, with a gap year between upper secondary and university studies. She met her partner and future husband at university. They had their first child when she was 24 and was just finishing her Bachelors degree. After a year's leave she returned to her studies and did a Master's in engineering. Although the timing of childbirth was very early compared with her peers, she did not suffer any setbacks in education or career-wise because of this as she had a very supportive husband and a family who provided support. When she finished her degree she got a job in the multinational and has been with the company since. She started off full time and had her second child two years after she got a permanent work contract. A year's maternity leave was followed by working 80 per cent time for a year before going back to full-time employment for two years. She was on maternity leave for the third child at the time of the interview.

Figure 4.5: Ingunn

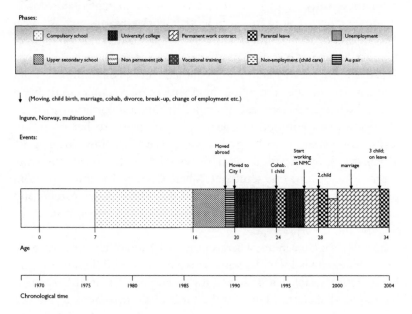

Ingunn expressed some thoughts about the timing of childbirth in her life course. Many of her friends and colleagues were having a first child when she was on her third pregnancy:

> 'I had my first child while at university and the second one right after I started working. When you are student you haven't had any considerable income to speak of, so that side of it didn't feel like a problem. I felt I was very flexible being a student. For me it was an ideal situation and it gave me additional motivation to get my degree fast and study efficiently.'

Although the timing of Ingunn's transition was 'off course' compared to her peers, she was very committed to her studies. Her supportive partner was also a student at the time, and parents and in-laws helped. Since the early 1990s the Norwegian study loan scheme has provided maternity leave benefit for student mothers in the form of a study loan being transformed to a grant if the requisite conditions are met. So for young people in Ingunn's situation, early timing of childbirth in the life course need not hamper their career prospects if other transitions, particularly education, follow an age normative route. However, the early transition to motherhood made for adult responsibilities earlier in life than her peers at university. And rather than having an income from employment, the family got by on study loans from the state.

Of these three cases Ingunn and Gro work in high-status, male-dominated occupations in a competitive work environment. Whereas Gro's transition to parenthood was carefully planned in relation to other transitions, Ingunn became a mother earlier in life without this having a negative impact on her education or subsequent career. Both came from middle-class families, providing them with extra resources to draw on beyond what the welfare state provided during this transition. Jorunn's transition to parenthood was very early compared to her peers, but less so compared to working-class women of her cohort (Lappegård, 1999). A lack of education and her having been a housewife for many years make Jorunn's case stand out. Where Gro and Ingunn came from privileged family backgrounds Jorunn did not, but her parents and in-laws nevertheless gave her the support that she saw as critical for her and her family.

For Norwegian parents, whatever the social and other circumstances, the welfare state helps in the transition to motherhood (Ellingsæter and Leira, 2004), a fact that does not always come across in the mothers' biographical accounts. This is still a form of knowledge that must be brought to bear on the interpretation of cases. These 'silences' may relate to the strong ideal of being independent and autonomous for young people in general (Brannen and Nilsen, 2002; Nilsen et al, 2002), and perhaps for young parents of middle-class background in particular (Brannen et al 2002). For those like Jorunn's husband who had a disability pension from the welfare state, this institution's positive impact is all the more undeniable.

Becoming a mother in a neoliberal and multicultural Western society: the UK

The existence of private schools and private healthcare alongside fairly well-funded public systems of education and health makes the UK a contrast to the Scandinavian countries on key areas of policy. In demographic terms, the average age at birth of the first child in Britain is 26, but with variations across social classes as in other countries. The UK, and especially London, is to a much greater extent than the other countries in the study a multicultural and multi-ethnic society.

Two studies were undertaken in the UK, one in a private sector finance company in the North of England and the other in a London social services department. The multi-ethnic composition is evident in the social services workforce in London. In the British context social workers have rather lower status than in Scandinavia (Brannen and Brockmann, 2005). In many instances the life courses of those who enter social services are less 'linear' than for those in private sector organisations. Social service workers, at all levels, often worked in other types of jobs before they started training/education in social work.

Public or subsidised housing has declined in all countries, in particular in the UK. The steep housing prices in London have led local authorities to set up schemes to help 'key workers' to buy homes in order to fill vacancies in fields of work such as social services. Concerns about the housing situation were found to be an issue in the UK interviews more than in the other countries.

Two UK cases illustrate aspects of the transition to motherhood, one working in a private sector company and another in social services. **Diane** is a 36-year-old manager in Peak, a private sector company. Her lifeline is linear in that trajectories and transitions follow in a 'normative' sequence. Diane comes from a white middle-class background. She went to university after upper secondary schooling and gained a degree in business studies. She met her husband, who works in finance, when they were both 22 when she first started working in the company. They cohabited and bought a house together and married when they were both 29.[6] They had their first child at 34.

At the time of the interview Diane was pregnant with the second child. The timing of childbirth was carefully planned: well-paid jobs, a house of their own, a lifestyle that included much travel abroad and other leisure activities were key considerations in the planning of parenthood. The general impression in Diane's case was one of a highly structured life course with carefully planned transitions.

Figure 4.6: Diane

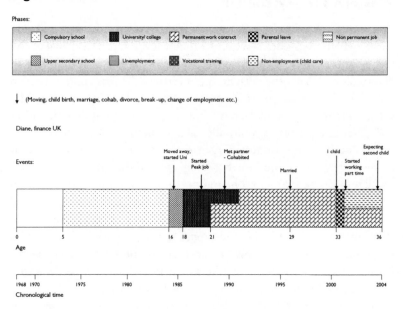

At 20 Diane thought she would have children earlier than in her mid-thirties:

> 'I think when you're 20 you think 30 is ancient don't you? I don't think you realise how quickly those 10 years just disappear into nothingness, but our big thing is we used to spend a lot on travel, we used to go away for weekends an awful lot, lots of European cities.'

The backgrounds and positions in occupational hierarchies of Diane and her husband made for a smooth transition to parenthood. Diane's case is not typical for the circumstances surrounding young women's transition to motherhood in general. It does, however, represent some aspects of the transition for the more privileged of our participants, particularly in north western European countries. Her transition pattern, like the Norwegian case, Gro, falls within the category of 'young adults' described in Chapter One. For this group of people life*style* is important since they have the spending power to consume beyond the 'consumption for basic needs' (Jones and Wallace, 1992; Brannen and Nilsen, 2005). For 'the young adults', the timing of the transitions to parenthood will not only be related to education, job and housing issues. For those who can afford an affluent lifestyle, choosing motherhood in many cases means that key features of lifestyle have to be achieved first. The transition is therefore not only one of deciding with reference to combining *work and family* and with basic material needs in mind. Equally important considerations are lifestyle and *leisure* activities.

Another case of transition from the UK highlights a different set of topics. Some of the social workers in the UK study who had migrated to Britain from Asian and African countries started their families while living with parents, in-laws or other relatives (Brannen and Brockmann, 2005).

Figure 4.7: Uche

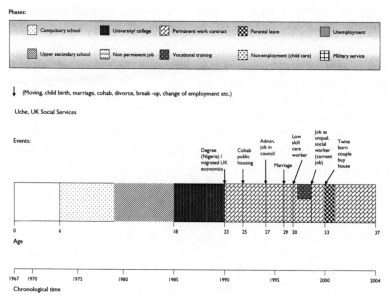

Uche is a 37-year-old unqualified social worker of African origin. She came to Britain in her early twenties and is married to a man from her birth country. They have two children aged three and four. She has a degree from a University in Africa but not in social work. She came to Britain to visit relatives and stayed on when she got a job as a clerical worker in the public sector. At 30 she changed jobs to become a social work assistant and has yet to find time to study for the social work qualification.

The couple would have liked to have had children earlier but she did not get pregnant until she was 33. Uche took four months' maternity leave at each birth and returned to work full time. Her husband is also a social worker, with a degree. She supported them both while he was at college. Her transition to parenthood was experienced as stressful because of the strained economic situation of the family. Before the birth of her first child her employer provided a small subsidy towards a deposit on a house. This happened under a scheme from the public sector described above. As Uche did not want to leave her children in the care of strangers, an elderly aunt (brought over from Africa) therefore moved in with them on a temporary basis to help with childcare.

Uche's trajectories have not followed a linear path. Her life course does not bear the mark of planning so evident in Diane's case. Uche moved away from the country where she was born and settled in work that did not demand a degree. The timing of childbirth was involuntarily postponed. In spite of having children rather late in life and thus experiencing an extended transition to parenthood, Uche falls into the category of 'early adulthood' since she had to support herself from an early age and was also the main breadwinner when her husband was working for his social work degree.

Comparing Uche and Diane, both had their children following marriage, a life course phase when the conditions were 'right'. But in contrast to Uche, Diane came from a white ethnic British middle-class family, and her education led her straight into a job where she currently holds a managerial position, while Uche did not find employment that matched her qualifications.

These two cases bring out aspects of social class very clearly. When Uche decided to try and become a mother, it was at a time in her life when finances were still difficult. Her decision was therefore taken *in spite of* the material limitations in their lives. For Uche the decision can therefore not be conceptualised as a lifestyle choice, but rather more of a life course decision. Diane's decision to become pregnant was, in contrast, taken under conditions of material affluence and a lifestyle where children would mean changing the established pattern of leisure activities.

Transition to motherhood in Southern Europe: Portugal

At the time of the Transitions study the main characteristics of the contemporary situation in Portugal was one of a weak welfare state, a weak economy but a massive rise in the level of qualifications in the population, although many leave school after 10 years. The level of poverty remains high, with 20 per cent of the population living below the poverty line. The percentage of women in the workforce has increased manifold over the past three decades with full-time work the norm. Childcare services have also greatly improved over the past decade, with many more crèches and childminders for young children.

Conditions for employees vary between the private and the public sectors – the public sector adheres to worker protection regulations, including measures for the benefit of working parents, to a greater extent than companies in the private sector (das Dores Guerreira et al, 2005).

The Portuguese cases demonstrate the same differences between the life courses of higher and lower educated interviewees in terms of timing of childbirth in relation to other life course transitions, as in the other countries. The system of education in Portugal is different from, for instance, the Scandinavian or the Dutch systems in that there is no study loan scheme. This in itself makes for highly class-segregated access to higher education. As we have addressed elsewhere (Nilsen et al, 2002), the opportunity structure for Portuguese young people, compared to Scandinavian youth, depends to a much higher extent on parental income and social class. Most young people live with their parents until they enter paid employment and often until marriage. For those who go to university their parents provide for them while studying, but some have part-time jobs to earn spending money. The few from working-class backgrounds who enter higher education often take evening classes and have full-time jobs in addition to their studies.

Young parents from middle-class families with higher education tend to have more extended linear trajectories than those of working-class background. The timing of childbirth is also later in the life course of the middle-class young. The Portuguese cases thus demonstrate that different types of 'linearity' are involved in middle-class and working-class trajectories (das Dores Guerreiro et al, 2005). Where a linear trajectory in middle-class lives includes a period of upper secondary and higher education followed by employment, marriage and children, in working-class lives it involves leaving school early and finding waged work as soon as possible, getting married and having a child. Linearity here refers to an unbroken line of activity where the working-class model follows a different pattern from that of the middle classes.

Alexandra is a 32-year-old mother of two with a degree in business studies. She comes from a middle-class background and her trajectory through the system of education is extended linear; upper secondary schooling was followed by university studies and short-term employment for half a year until she got a permanent work contract with the private sector company. Like most Portuguese young people from middle-class backgrounds, she lived with her parents until she got married, which she did when she and her partner were both 25. Her husband has been her long-term, and only, boyfriend. Their first child was born a year after the wedding. The pregnancy was not planned but she was happy with this since she says she would not have liked to have a child late in life. Her second child was, at the time of the interview, 22 months old. About the timing of marriage she says:

> 'We had both worked for two years already and we had some money, it wasn't that much but it was enough. We had actually bought a house and were making repairs there so the decision to get married was very natural.'

Figure 4.8: Alexandra

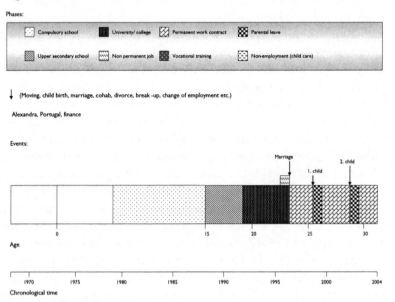

Phases:

Compulsory school | University/college | Permanent work contract | Parental leave

Upper secondary school | Non permanent job | Vocational training | Non-employment (child care)

↓ (Moving, child birth, marriage, cohab, divorce, break-up, change of employment etc.)

Alexandra, Portugal, finance

Events:

When she first got pregnant she was concerned about her career as the work pattern in the finance company was 'seasonal', involving the yearly auditing of company accounts. She was worried that the timing of childbirth would coincide with the most hectic period in the company's year, and was happy when this did not happen.

Alexandra had a lot of help and support from her parents when the first child was born as her mother looked after him during the day. The family income was high enough to have paid help in the house. Her husband did not, however, take much part in either childminding or housework.

Alexandra's life course is similar to that of most young people of middle-class backgrounds in her birth cohort, and she is representative of what we described above as having had a 'long period of youth'. Living with her parents until marriage and then moving into a separate household with her husband is the norm in Portugal. The average age at birth of the first child is also lower than in the Northern European countries.

Figure 4.9: Dália

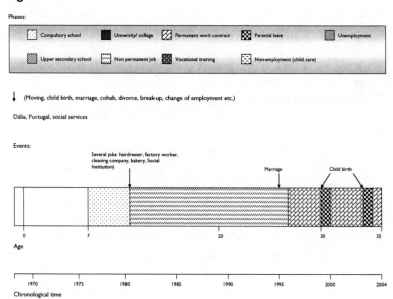

Dália, Portugal, social services

Dália, a 38-year-old mother of two, illustrates a short, linear working-class trajectory. She left school at 13 having completed what was compulsory schooling at the time. After having had a series of non-skilled short-term jobs (cleaning, factory work etc) from the time she left school, she is now a care worker with the social services looking after elderly clients. She got married at 28 and has two children aged five and two. Her husband was, at the time of the interview, unemployed. About the transition to parenthood, Dália says about the second child:

> 'After my son I thought no more but he started telling us he wanted a sister. We thought about it and there he got his sister! It's difficult but now we feel really happy with our little one!'

Dália's trajectories are in the strict sense linear. However, the series of jobs in which she had been employed were all on short-term contracts; only when she joined social services did she get a permanent work contract. Her transition from youth to adulthood falls in the category of 'early adulthood' as she had to provide for herself from an early age. The life course was marked by insecurity related to employment and income. She went back to full-time employment after the statutory maternity leave for both children. She received a lot of support and help from her parents, who lived with them when Dália was working. Her husband did not take much of a part in looking after the children or the housework, even though he was unemployed, something Dália complained about. The system of networks around Dália seems to be composed of women across generations helping and supporting each other in complex everyday situations.

Alexandra's first child was not planned and she was relieved because the birth did not coincide with a hectic period at work. For Dália this did not pose a problem since her work was not a 'career'. She was satisfied with her situation, however, and considered herself lucky to have a permanent work contract in a job she found rewarding on many levels. For Alexandra the job was also important because she thought of it as a career.[7] Being absent from work during a period when her skills were most needed could hinder her future career prospects. The trajectories of these two women illustrate different types of linearity – the former more extended than the latter – that are strongly associated with social class.

The situation for the Portuguese women's transition to motherhood, however different their circumstances, was eased by the support provided by their mothers and female relatives. In Portugal, as in most other countries, practical support with care work is generally a female issue. Family support in the general sense is wide-ranging in that it is made up of several elements with financial assistance important. However, most of the everyday intergenerational support involves largely female kin networks. Moreover, this type of support network is evident across social classes in the Portuguese context.

Comparing transitions to motherhood across countries

As stated in Chapter Three the interviewees in the Transitions project were all mothers and fathers who were selected because they represented cases of working parents in specific organisational settings across particular countries. A typological framework for describing the overall pattern of transition from youth to adulthood that we developed in an earlier study (Brannen et al, 2002; Nilsen et al, 2002) has proved useful in discussing transitions to motherhood. In this chapter we have combined this with the standard life course vocabulary which refers to linearity in trajectories and timing in transitions. Where the life course follows a 'normative route' through the age-graded systems of education and in relation to average age of birth of the first child in the national context, the trajectories follow short or extended linear patterns. Where this is not the case, we have named the patterns of trajectories 'non-linear' or 'semi-linear'.

What the analysis of cases in this chapter suggests is that the *timing* of the transition to motherhood for many is an event that is planned in relation to other life course transitions, mainly education and employment. For those who became pregnant without having planned to, the phase of life and thus its relationship to other life course transitions when this happened affects other contingent trajectories, as the Norwegian cases of Ingunn and Jorunn illustrate. These cases also highlight how different resources in the form of welfare state provisions and family support are context-dependent and have an impact on the trajectories.

Where this transition is the result of careful planning, there are also differences in the cases associated with several layers in the context. In the case of the Portuguese accountant, Alexandra, the timing of childbirth was not only important in relation to other life course transitions; her work was important in that her job involved different levels of intensity over the year, some periods being more stressful than others. She was concerned about taking maternity leave during the busiest time of year as this would have been frowned upon by her employer. The overall timing of the transition did in this case follow a standard pattern for Portuguese young people of middle-class background.

Another aspect of timing is related to those areas of life that are considered a priority when thinking of having a child. In the UK case of Diane, a middle-class manager in a finance company, the considerations she and her husband took into account were as much related to lifestyle and leisure activities as with other fundamental concerns of housing and adequate income. Consumption was important to Diane and her husband, suggesting differences between more privileged parents and those who were less privileged in that the former could afford to think of life course transitions in terms of *lifestyle choices*. Those who said most explicitly that the timing of parenthood was carefully planned were those with higher education and high-income jobs, as the similar Norwegian case of Gro demonstrates.

Discussions of the timing of transitions have demonstrated that the typologies describing the transition from youth to adulthood introduced in Chapter One are context-sensitive. The typologies were constructed on the basis of data from Northern and Southern Europe and based on 'standard' markers of adulthood as described above. One such important marker is setting up an independent household and being able to provide for oneself. Cases from Bulgaria illustrate difficulties with finding independent housing for young families. Thus in many cases a form of semi-independence from the family of origin exists. This is not surprising since Bulgaria is the country in the study that has most recently undergone profound changes in its economy, its political sphere and social life. When the public sector and hence the health system and welfare state provisions became severely weakened, family support became all the more important. There are thus differences between countries with regard to the involvement of *the extended family* in the transition to parenthood. In Southern and Eastern Europe family seems to play a bigger role in young couples' lives than in countries in Northern Europe. Only a few in the UK, Sweden, Norway and the Netherlands mention family as key sources of support at this transition, for childcare in particular. The Norwegian case of Jorunn illustrates how the family was very close – her parents lived in the same neighbourhood and they were an important source of support. Overall, however, in Western Europe kin and family seem to provide less everyday and 'hands on' support than in Southern and Eastern Europe. The Bulgarian case, Rosa, demonstrates how the transition to adulthood was made smooth by parents who helped her find a job, secured housing and provided childcare in addition to the public kindergarten. The other Bulgarian case, Nelly, illustrates some important differences in family support that are related to the wider contextual differences between countries. Although Nelly already had a university degree when her first child was born, the situation in which she found herself became very stressful, with her husband away a lot and considerable pressure at work. The option she chose in those circumstances is referred to as a 'typical Bulgarian' decision – she left the child with her parents during the weekdays.

In Portugal the extended family is also important during the transition to motherhood although not to the same extent as in Bulgaria. Some parents live with young couples for a period of time to provide help and support in the phase where assistance and childcare are needed. However, as the cases analysed in this chapter have demonstrated, family support in the form of childcare in both Eastern and Southern Europe tend to be based on generational networks of *women* in families. Only in very few instances are men involved in the day-to-day care of their grandchildren.

The cases across these four countries demonstrate how *material resources* – both individual in terms of social class, level of education and income, and institutional support provided in the form of affordable access to housing, education, childcare, maternity leave and so forth – influence the timing of the transition to motherhood and the subsequent experiences of it. The higher the level of education the later in the life course the transition to parenthood tends to occur. Where there are instances of an early transition to motherhood and higher education, as in the case of Norwegian Ingunn, resources provided by middle-class parents, a supportive partner and a study loan scheme become important for a smooth transition that does not have a negative impact on the later occupational career. Welfare state provisions play an important role in the lives of young people in Western Europe, notably the Scandinavian countries. The strong discourse of 'autonomy and independence' that is evident among young people in these countries sustain a belief in their own solutions and underplay notions of dependency on others.

Social class is important for the transition to motherhood in all the countries in our study. However, the comparative analysis has demonstrated that the impact of class must be considered within the overall resource situation relating to the institutional fabrics of different societies. Where Alexandra's (the Portuguese accountant) mother helped with childminding during the day for the new mother, a similar case from the same class background would be less common in the UK or Scandinavia.

Most of the mothers interviewed for this study made the transition to motherhood on completing other life course transitions such as higher education and having established a relationship with a partner in a household separate from the family of origin. In this chapter we have examined and compared variations between the countries on this transition. Rather than highlight aspects of personal choices, which is a crucial component in life course transitions and trajectory development, we have sought to demonstrate the interplay between structure and agency. Cross-national comparative studies can show very clearly how structural circumstances inform and affect the trajectories of individual life courses in general and the transition to motherhood in particular. Although there are many similarities in the cases across countries, the great variety of transition patterns and trajectories demonstrate how a grounded life course analysis teases out nuances that many other perspectives emphasising notions of late modernity and de-standardisation of life courses (Beck and Beck-Gernsheim, 1995) miss out on. An approach that is attentive to the peculiarities of the layers of context that individual lives are lived within has proved useful for demonstrating the complexities of these transitions across countries and how these must be taken into consideration for a deeper understanding of the processes involved.

Notes

[1] Housing markets vary between the countries, and although some countries have fewer opportunities for renting since the deregulation of the housing markets (Balchin, 1996), most young people who move out of the parental home for the first time move into rented housing. On establishing a family, however, there are variations in degree of home ownership.

[2] This is explained in Bulgarian research by the generous policies towards parents during the communist regime. Policies have since then changed so that parents no longer get subsidised housing and have less job protection. The labour market has also changed so that secure jobs are fewer and harder to get (Kovacheva and Matev, 2005 p 14).

[3] Many of the other employees in the agency had come to social work without the relevant qualifications. Their personal transitions have been interrupted when the country started its transition to a market economy. They have left jobs in engineering and agriculture when the factories and large cooperatives closed down and they found openings in the new field of welfare provision and only after that they received training in social work (Kovacheva, 2009).

[4] GDI (Gender Development Index) and the GEM (Gender Empowerment Measure) are both used by the UN as indicators of gender equity in societies. Whereas the first measures gender differences on much the same data as the

HDI (Human Development Index), life expectancy, education level etc, the GEM is calculated by measuring the percentage of women in parliament, in leadership and managerial positions (www.un.org).

[5] The majority of women in this older generation left school after compulsory education at 15, had a job for a few years before they got married and became housewives supported by their husbands (Wærness, 1982).

[6] Housing prices in that region of the UK were affordable at the time and it was quite common for young people in their twenties to buy a house (Smithson and Lewis, 2004). A period-specific aspect of this is also the encouragement of home ownership during the Thatcher era and the selling off of council housing through the 'Right to Buy' scheme.

[7] See Nilsen (2011) for a discussion of careers versus non-career types of jobs and differerences in impact on work–family issues.

FIVE

Comparing transitions to fatherhood across contexts

Lars Plantin, Margareta Bäck-Wiklund, Siyka Kovacheva and Maria das Dores Guerreiro

Introduction: transitions to fatherhood in context

Expectations of men as parents have changed over the last century, from the traditional position of the distant breadwinner to a more equal and nurturing father (Plantin et al, 2003; Edwards et al, 2009). As well as breadwinning, caring activities and time spent with children – forms of emotional work – are important dimensions of fathering that can have an impact on child development and family harmony (Coltrane, 1996; Lamb and Lewis, 2004; Dermott, 2008).

As discussed in Chapter Two, European society has been marked by major social change over the past 50 years: the rise of the Women's Movement, an increase in two-income families alongside increases in women's labour force participation, the introduction of parental leave, and shifting marriage and divorce patterns. In this context there is a good deal of discussion about the 'new fatherhood' that has become a political issue in some countries (Hobson and Morgan, 2002). Men's increasing interest in fathering has been identified by researchers in different countries (Brandth and Kvande, 2003; Duyvendak and Stavenuiter, 2004; Brannen and Nilsen, 2006). For example, Hobson and Fahlén (2009), drawing on the European Social Survey (ESS) for 2004, show how the vast majority of fathers think that reconciling work and family life is a high priority. Many fathers also wanted to reduce their working hours substantially in favour of more time with their families, although this was not always reflected in actual behaviour. However, despite whether men work full time or reduce their work time, they were still deeply emotionally engaged in their children. In Miller's (2011) interview study the men reported very strong ties to their children and showed a greater commitment to daily practices of hands-on caring than ever before. These attitudes have also gradually started to affect organisations' policies and practices for fathers (Haas and Hwang, 2009). However, in recent years arguments about the 'business case', emphasising efficiency and organisational change, have changed the debate:'greedy organisations' are challenging both modern motherhood and fatherhood.[1]

There are significant differences among welfare policies aimed at fathers between the countries in the study (Fagnani et al, 2004; see Chapter Two, this volume). Some countries have recently developed extensive welfare support for fathers, equal to that for mothers, while others still support mothers as the primary caregivers. However, the policies relevant here are those that were in place in the countries at the time of the fathers' first transition to parenthood, the focus of this chapter.

Reflecting the focus of Chapter Four on the transition to motherhood, the transition to fatherhood is discussed in relation to other life course transitions such as school leaving, gainful employment, moving out of the parental household and cohabitation/marriage. The chapter also highlights dominant national cultures. It analyses individual decisions about becoming a father. Lifelines are analysed and set in the contexts of national age-based transitions relating to systems of education, average age at birth of the first child and so forth. Interpretations and reflections provided by the interviewees about the course of their lives are analysed and compared.

Three national contexts are in focus in this chapter: Sweden, Bulgaria and Portugal. They represent the three types of regions identified in Chapter Two: Northern, Southern and Eastern Europe. Other contextual information relating to the transition to fatherhood is drawn on where relevant.

Discourses about fatherhood often coincide with discourses about gender equality and equity as they are located in particular national cultures and values. In Sweden gender equality was declared a national goal in the 1970s and has been part of a public debate and political agenda ever since. In Portugal concerns about gender equality and equity along with extended rights for working parents emerged after the 1974 revolution. New family laws defined equal rights for couples. However, the father's changing role debate is recent – only in 2000 were fathers entitled to five days of fully paid paternity leave on the birth of a child. In Bulgaria equality between genders was part of the communist ideology but the division of labour in families remained traditional, with mothers doing more care work and domestic chores than fathers. This picture is also confirmed in the fourth wave of the ESS (ESS, 2010), with Sweden among the countries with the highest acceptance of gender equality, Bulgaria at the opposite end with the most traditional gender role attitudes and Portugal in the middle.

Transitions to fatherhood in a Northern European welfare state: Sweden

In Sweden transitions are gendered. Men join the labour market earlier than women and work full time far more often. They are also less eager than women to have a child and a family of their own (Ungdomsstyrelsen, 2003). Consequently, on average they are three years older than women when they have their first child (SCB, 2009). The dual-earner family model, usually with two or more children, is the main family pattern.[2] In spite of institutional support for both men and women, a 'light' version of gender equality is practised among many young parents. The majority of fathers take parental leave but mothers are still the main carers, and fathers use about a quarter of the days available of the parental insurance (Försäkringskassan, 2010).

In the analysis of the transition to fatherhood we have identified different patterns in relation to other life course trajectories. Thus *a normative age-graded* (or *linear*) life course for young people in Sweden is to move out of the parental home at the average age of 19 after completing upper secondary school and then to proceed to university and live in a separate household (Ungdomsstyrelsen, 2003). After graduation they take up employment, maybe cohabit with one or two partners in succession, before they have their first child, which they do between the ages of 27 to 31. A parallel path can be found for those with no university education and consequently a longer phase in waged work.

Many young people follow *non-linear* educational and employment trajectories. They spend some years exploring different jobs and go travelling abroad before starting a family. New patterns are emerging for those who take one or more gap years between upper secondary school and university and sometimes also gap years between graduation and employment. Young people who go to university usually do so within five years after upper secondary; on graduation they get a job, cohabit, buy or rent a house or apartment and have their first child. Traditionally most young people go through education without much economic support from their parents but instead rely on temporary work and/or study loans from the state.

The non-linear patterns illustrate how the period between upper secondary and university, and the time between entry to the labour market and parenthood have been extended for some groups. Many young people start out with a somewhat vague idea about the future and wish to explore their individuality, different partners, temporary low-skilled jobs and sometimes also wish to travel the world. Both careers and parenthood are 'put on hold' in order to pursue individual wishes as well as to comply with institutional requirements (Brannen et al, 2002). After such a 'long period of youth' (Nilsen et al, 2002), employment careers and family formation are set on a more traditional track. The establishment of a relationship may be contingent and processual. However, the timing of the transition to parenthood is often coordinated with career demands and with finding a stable economic and housing situation. This is illustrated in men's reflections over which conditions are 'right' for the transition to fatherhood.

A *linear* pattern of trajectories is age-specific and has no gap years after upper secondary or higher education. Individuals move out of the parental home into separate accommodation (most often rented), have a series of different jobs, cohabit, have a child. Having a child is often unplanned – it 'just happens' after moving in with a partner – but is welcomed when it does. After the child, parents engage in more deliberate planning and decision making.

Figure 5.1: Linus

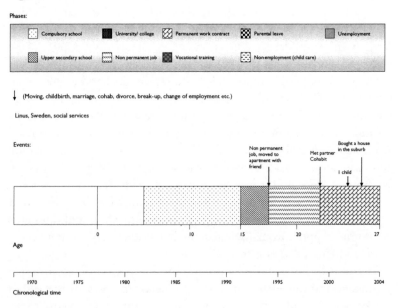

Linus represents a linear trajectory. He was born in 1977 in a working-class family living in a working-class neighbourhood. He left school at 17 in 1995 with two years of upper secondary schooling (a vocational school for carpenters), a choice that did not make him eligible for higher education although he never considered this an option. Just after he finished school he moved into an apartment with a friend and got a job as a carpenter for a year. He then had several different jobs until 1999 when he got a permanent job as a caretaker/driver in a social services unit. At the age of 24 he moved to another apartment, this time with his girlfriend who was a pre-school teacher.[3] Two years later their son was born and the couple bought a terraced house in a suburb. It was located in an area with good childcare facilities and close to his partner's work.

Linus' transition between youth and adulthood can be described in terms of the category 'early adulthood'. His reflections about the transition to fatherhood are expressed in the following way:

> 'Becoming a father felt very far away … but on the other hand I still had the same feeling when we actually were "pregnant". But over all I think it suited us perfectly when it was a reality.'

> 'You were 26 years … was that a perfect age for you to become a father?'

> 'Yes, even if it wasn't planned.'

> 'Did you fail to use contraceptives?'

> 'Yes, I think it was like that….'

> 'So it was very sudden?'

> 'Yes, but it wasn't uncomfortable in any ways. We decided rather quickly to keep the child and yes I think it was the right time for us. I also felt mature and knew I had met the right girl.'

Although the pregnancy was not really planned they went ahead with it and were happy to have the child. Linus' feeling of being mature and having met the right partner added to the positive experience of becoming a father without having gone through a phase of careful planning.

Figure 5.2: Paul

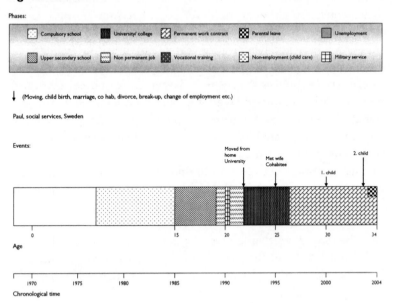

Phases:

Compulsory school	University/ college	Permanent work contract	Parental leave	Unemployment
Upper secondary school	Non permanent job	Vocational training	Non-employment (child care)	Military service

↓ (Moving, child birth, marriage, co hab, divorce, break-up, change of employment etc.)

Paul, social services, Sweden

Paul represents a non-linear trajectory. He was born in 1970 into a middle-class family. His father was a priest that in many ways seems to have affected Paul's transition to adulthood. In upper secondary school he did a three-year programme that qualified him for university.[4]

He left school at 18 and had different low-skilled jobs, spent a year in the military service as a conscientious objector and did not move out of his parents' house until the age of 20. Then he moved to another town and got work in an organisation for troubled youth run by the church. At 23 he started studying at university to become a social worker.[5] He had been working with young people and wanted to continue this type of work and was also influenced by a friend in his choice of career. He married in 1996 when he was 25 years old and had just graduated. His wife graduated the same year as a teacher at the age of 22. To get married in Sweden at this age is regarded as relatively early, but Paul and his wife's decision is related to their religious convictions and active church membership. After four years they bought a house in a relatively expensive suburb. They both had permanent jobs and could afford to buy a house in the same type of surroundings they were used to from childhood. They chose an area where the sister of Paul's wife and her family lived. Living close to relatives offered them opportunities for babysitters in the future. Paul and his wife waited for six years before they decided to have their first child. His transition to adulthood is similar to some of the cases in Chapter Four (Diane and Gro) and bears resemblance to the 'young adults' category described earlier.

Paul's reflections on the transition to fatherhood and 'a traditional family' are expressed in the following way:"Unconsciously it was there … the future looked like that: to have children, family and a house."

But even if he knew 'the model' and accepted it, he still could not say *why* they decided to have children. They discussed it and planned it but still he hesitated to answer the question:"A good question but I don't know, actually."

However, the conditions felt right as "both of us had finished our educations and we had bought the house".

While both Linus and Paul ended up with the same 'model' of adulthood – "children, family and a house", they clearly adopted different approaches and ways into this situation. The whole interview with Linus shows how building a family and becoming a parent was "natural" for him, something that "just happens". Paul, on the other hand, seems to have put more planning into his approach to parenthood. He was more than 30 years old when he had his first child and he spent all the years between 20 and 30 trying out different jobs and getting a higher education, meeting a girl, getting married, establishing himself in a job and buying a house.

These patterns are also found in other studies on men's transition to fatherhood and relate to social class. In an earlier study of Swedish fathers by Plantin (2007) it was found that fathers in working-class households often saw fatherhood as a way of creating meaning in their lives, and saw the process of becoming a parent as an explicit aspiration to establishing something 'natural', taken for granted and predictable. Fathers in middle-class households, on the other hand, considered fatherhood to involve a different phase of life: a reflexive project and something that needed to be thoroughly planned. In practice, these different views of fatherhood were illustrated by the finding that the working-class fathers often had a much shorter period of 'self-exploration', and hence had a transition phase between youth and adulthood that fell into the category of 'early adulthood' (Nilsen et al, 2002). They also became fathers at an earlier age and did not plan for a long parental leave as the middle-class men did.

Transition to fatherhood in a Southern European country: Portugal

The system of education in Portugal is different from the Scandinavian countries in that there is no study loan scheme. This in itself makes for a highly class-segregated access to higher education – only 29 per cent of the cohort covered by this study had upper secondary education (OECD, 2010), while in Sweden this figure was 90 per cent. The opportunity structure for Portuguese young people compared to Scandinavian youth depends to a much higher extent on parental income and social class. Most young people live with their parents until they enter paid employment and often until marriage (Guerreiro et al , 2004). Less than 4 per cent of young people live alone. For those who go to university their parents provide for them but some have part-time jobs for spending money. Those from working-class backgrounds who enter higher education often take evening classes and have a full-time job in addition to studying.

As discussed in Chapter Four, Portuguese *extended linear* transition patterns to adulthood include young people who take higher education and who tend to live with their parents while in education and until they marry and start a family. Those who do not attend higher education tend to leave home earlier when they find employment to support themselves. The latter also demonstrate linearity in their work and education trajectories, with short or truncated transition phases. Some routes into social work careers suggest changes in Portuguese society that have opened up for social mobility. Such patterns often involve non-linear educational trajectories, as in the case of Gaspar.

Gaspar is a 37-year-old trained psychologist who comes from a working-class background. He works in social services. He left school at 16 and had several unskilled jobs for many years. As shown in the lifeline, at 18 he started upper secondary education via evening classes and at 25 he started his Master's degree at university, still working full time and doing evening classes. This pattern of education is becoming more frequent among people of working-class background. There is no study loan scheme in Portugal, and those who come from family backgrounds where parents cannot support them through university have no option but to support themselves with waged work through education. However, Gaspar lived in his parents' house until he met his partner in 1998 and bought a house with her. He is therefore an example of what we have previously described as a 'long period of youth' in terms of his living with his parents until moving in with a partner. The fact that he earned his own wage is, however, a factor that puts his transition pattern into the 'early adulthood' category.[6]

Figure 5.3: Gaspar

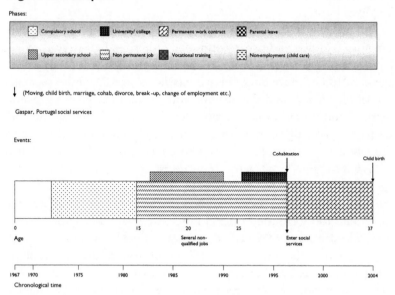

At the time of the interview the couple had an eight-month-old child. About the timing of childbirth Gaspar said:

> 'We were both on temporary work contracts, in what concerns professional situation.... I also thought about age, and we both had a natural desire ... we postponed it a little, but then we decided it wasn't necessary to wait for the ideal conditions, maybe they'd never come, so we decided to have a child.'

Gaspar became a father at 37, late in life by Portuguese standards, but his case is illustrative for several reasons; first, because he is a man of working-class background who followed the only option open for young people of this background to gain higher education, which is combining full-time work with evening classes to gain a degree and thus achieve a better paid job with a higher status. His case is also illustrative in that as a father he was not entitled to much in the way of paid parental leave.[7] The gender role structure in Portugal is more traditional than is the case in the two Scandinavian countries. While the transition to parenthood is gendered in all countries, the case of Gaspar illustrates some aspects that are particular to the Portuguese case.

When asked: 'When you were young, did you plan to marry and have children?', Gaspar answered: "Everybody wants to get married and have kids!"

The answer refers to normative expectations, not to his own intentions. However, Gaspar postponed fatherhood far beyond what is common in Portugal. He had had several girlfriends but only at the age of 32 did he move out of his parents' home and establish a separate household in a rented flat shared with his partner. They were not married and waited to have a child for several years. He says he and his partner gave up waiting for a more stable situation in which they thought it 'right' to have a baby. But he also considered his age and that of his wife an important factor in the decision – they wanted to be the age of "parents and not grandparents". They bought a flat just before the baby was born, as Gaspar said, "to give the baby more comfort, and for parents too". Housing prices in the area where they settled down were affordable and they had access to good public transport. Gaspar and his partner could not count on support from relatives, as none of the grandparents lived nearby and the child was in a nursery while they were at work. However, he would have liked to have had family help with the caring: "No institutional arrangement is able to replace the family, without any doubt."

Figure 5.4: João

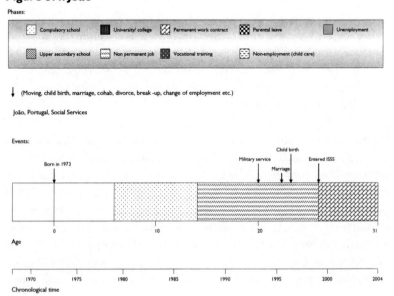

João, a 32-year-old social services driver, is typical of the educational trajectory of nearly one third of Portuguese working-class men (das Dores Guerreiro et al, 2005). He left school at 15 without a secondary education diploma. He decided to train as an electrician and started work and training in this occupation. Later on he had to abandon this for health reasons. After military service he had several jobs as a driver. João has been in his current occupation at the social services catering distribution since he was 27. He lived with his parents until he married and became a father very early, when he was 23. The transition to fatherhood was not planned – his now nine-year-old daughter was born shortly after the couple moved in together. He and his partner split up when the daughter was three. His daughter stayed with him and he was a lone parent for two years until he moved in with his father and an older sister of his, which was still his family situation at the time of the interview. Unlike most Portuguese men he was deeply involved in housework and childcare:

> '... [while I was alone with my daughter] I used to do the laundry and the chores. Now I cook and during my week break days I bring my daughter and my niece to and from school.'

João's life course and his current circumstances illustrate some structural conditions of Portuguese society with its lack of institutional support for single-parent families. If a single parent needs support, especially with childcare, he or she often shares in a three-generation household.

João's life course is one in which *contingencies* seem to define his trajectories and transitions. He started a family and became a father without planning it. Later his partner left him and he became a single parent. After the separation the stress of coping as a lone parent with a three-year-old and working hard to make ends meet and pay the mortgage caused him to have a serious car accident – he fell asleep at the wheel. During the sick leave period he fell behind with his mortgage payments and had to sell the apartment and move in with his father. All these events were unplanned, unexpected and unpredictable, and forced João to make decisions that resulted in a different course of life than he had anticipated when he was younger. His transition from youth to adulthood can be described as 'early adulthood' in spite of his living at home with his family until the age of 23 and having moved back there at the time of the interview. He supported himself and his daughter but lived in a shared household with his wider family.

Both João and Gaspar come from working-class backgrounds in a national context that does not provide much in the way of support for low-income families. While Gaspar did upper secondary and higher education as evening classes while working full time and got his degree later in life than his middle-class peers, João did not pursue such options and became a father unplanned at an early age. His subsequent phase as a lone parent was a hard time in which he had difficulty making ends meet.

Gaspar's trajectory indicates careful long-term planning – he manages to take advantage of those opportunities that exist for young people who have no families to support them through higher education. The housing support given by his parents was, however, a great help to him in achieving his current status as a professional employee. João did not seem to have had the same level or type of support, although he did live with his parents until he moved in with the child's mother. Moving back in with his father and his sister after he became a lone parent is, however, evidence of a supportive family under conditions of need. In contrast to Gaspar's planning of life course transitions, João's transitions are characterised by contingencies and unfortunate circumstances that have left him in a more vulnerable situation than Gaspar. However, with the pooling of family resources, three generations of João's family managed to get by and support each other. Gaspar experienced upward social mobility through taking a degree. He and his partner decided to have a child in spite of the life course timing not being as optimal to do – the 'age issue': delayed marriage, late studying and taking time to become economically secure. Living in a two-income household made it possible for the family to have paid childcare, although they would have preferred family to look after the child.

These cases illustrate how the opportunity structure in Portugal is very difficult for young people from low-income families. They also demonstrate different attitudes and practices towards becoming a father in a society that is characterised by conservative gender roles, as discussed in Chapter Four. Lone fathers are rare in Portugal. Moreover, whereas in Scandinavian countries lone parents can get help and support from the welfare state, for João his family was the only source of help in his situation. On his own he could not manage both to work and to look after his daughter. In the household João did some cooking and also did the shopping, trying not "to become a weight" for his sister, who in turn helped out with bringing his daughter to the nursery and picking her up in the afternoon.

Compared with Gaspar, João's life as a father was not the result of careful planning but nevertheless he assumed the role of involved father, even if he had to find support from his extended family. Gaspar, on the other hand, planned to become a father and complained about the lack of a family nearby for childcare support.

Becoming a parent in a post-communist country in transition: Bulgaria

Under the communist regime the normative pattern of transitions to employment was to have a contract with a state enterprise while still at school or university, ensuring a stipend and work placement on graduation (Wallace and Kovacheva, 1998; Chapter Two, this volume). At present both high and low educated young people start working while they are still in full-time education and then have a period of precarious jobs, most often in the informal economy (Mitev, 2005). Still, according to Eurostat (2009), Bulgarian youth enter employment later than the EU average. The statutory minimum school leaving age is still 16, as it was during communism, but in the first decade after liberalisation student numbers at universities doubled. Former state restrictions were abolished and old universities expanded by establishing branches in smaller towns and many new private universities opened (Kovacheva, 2001). Student stipends are still available but to a limited number of young people with a much lower value than before and the new loan schemes are still not well developed and are rarely used.

This mixture of old and new trends is demonstrated in the analysis of the trajectories of two young fathers, both of whom were employed at a social work unit. One of the fathers only had compulsory schooling and the other was a university graduate. As discussed in Chapters Two and Three, biographies are formed by institutional structures of opportunity and constraints but are also the result of individual agency. Becoming fathers and employees, young men attach meaning to their actions and develop their aspirations and own self-concepts.

A non-linear trajectory of a young man with low qualifications in the Bulgarian context is represented by a 29-year-old working-class man, **Miro**, a driver at a social work agency. He comes from a working-class family. His parents divorced when Miro was nine and he went to live with his grandparents. Miro had not profited from the growing trend towards mass university education in Bulgaria largely due to a lack of family resources and an early transition to fatherhood. He is a father of two children (one and three years old). Leaving school at 17 with no qualifications he started working for his grandparents' small business and held a number of temporary jobs after doing the obligatory military service for two years. While struggling to establish himself in the labour market, Miro continued living with his grandparents. During communism his transition would have been shorter and linear – with a direct passage from school to work. Under the new liberalised labour market with high unemployment of young people, they no longer have the employment opportunities possible under the centrally planned economy.

Figure 5.5: Miro

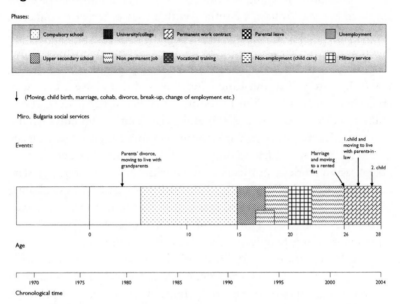

Miro, Bulgaria social services

Miro met his partner when he was 24 and one year later they moved in together renting a small flat. When his partner became pregnant they married and he applied for a job with a permanent work contract. He had been with social services for two years. His wife comes from a middle-class background and holds a university degree. She has never been in waged work and is currently studying part time for a law degree. Miro and his partner's transition to parenthood happened at a time when the social security system and health insurance were being reformed in Bulgaria. Miro describes his employment trajectory thus:

> 'I was trying out various options. My grandparents' business did not last long and anyway it was just very small. After the army I did not want to go into the shop and they closed it. I was deceived by one businessman having worked for him for a month without pay. Then in another job they did not

give me a contract and paid much less than promised. Then I
found a job as a truck driver and was often on long trips....
I could afford the rent [of a flat] and restaurants every week
... and all that but this is not a life for a family man.'

The transition to fatherhood for Miro involved a change in employment
to a low-paid but secure job in the state sector with a regular working
schedule and more time to spend with his wife and children. Becoming
a father unexpectedly like João, the Portuguese social services driver,
Miro took this responsibility very seriously and wanted to get involved
in childcare to a much greater degree than his own father had done.
At the age of 20 he had not thought about a family and children, nor
had he any definite plans about a job and career. At the interview
he was spending a lot of time every evening and weekends with his
children and wanted to do more of the housework when they moved
to independent housing:

'The children changed my life. I became much more serious
and responsible. Before that I had no responsibilities, I was
thinking only about myself. I am so happy now having my
children. I don't regret having them in any way.'

At the time of the interview the young family lived in one room in
his wife's parents' house as they were no longer able to pay the rent
and maintenance expenses of the small flat. They were given another
flat by Miro's parents but it required repairs and upkeep that the young
family could not afford. As in the forthcoming case of Simon and like
the Portugese case of João, it was common for parents in Bulgaria to
provide housing for their children, either providing an independent
dwelling or sharing their own flat or house with them.

Miro's transition pattern is also gendered in that he was the main
breadwinner and that he had not taken any parental leave. He also
thought it 'natural' that his wife should take care of the children until
they turned five. Yet due to his low-paid job in the public sector he
could not really provide for the family without the support from his
parents and parents-in-law. His transition to parenthood was part
of his 'early adulthood' transition since he had had to take on adult
responsibilities in the form of fatherhood from an early age.

Simon is a 30-year-old high-status social worker with a university
diploma in social pedagogy. He comes from a middle-class family and
had a linear educational trajectory. While studying at the university he
received a student grant for academic achievement and lived with his

parents. The grant was rather low but sharing the flat with his parents allowed him not to work while studying.[8] Thus Simon's transition from youth to adulthood fits into the category of a 'long period of youth'.

Figure 5.6: Simon

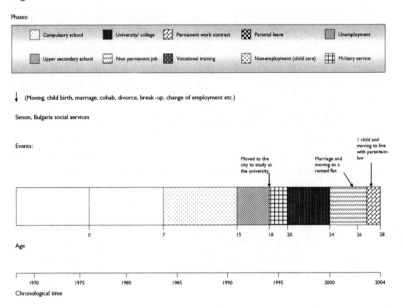

Simon got involved in voluntary work and on graduation was employed by an NGO:

> 'We started as a very young team in the beginning ... and were very ambitious wanting everything to be well organised. We even started before the premises were ready and worked in the street for a time ... I have mixed feelings now. In organisational terms things were not very good, many things were not clear.... Besides we had a flexible schedule and had to work during weekends. I was looking for a state job where things are settled down and there is more security.'

Simon left this job after three years and worked in a supermarket for two years until he found a job in a social work unit. At first he had a temporary contract as a social worker and commuted to work in a small town near his city for six months. At the time of the interview he had a permanent contract and a place at one of the seven units in the city. His entry into the labour market occurred at a time of high unemployment. Simon felt lucky that he had managed to find a permanent job relevant to his qualifications. He felt determined to succeed and make a career in his occupation.

His education to employment transition was not affected by his transition to fatherhood to the same extent as was the case for Miro – Simon followed his ambition "to establish himself as a professional in the social sphere". He was reasonably happy with his job situation although he judged his income as insufficient to support a family.

> Simon planned his family transition in a rather traditional way, so that he became a father at the age of 29 after he had settled down in his permanent job at the agency. At the age of 20 he was doing his obligatory military service and had the idea "When released from the army to be accepted at the university and then eventually to find a job and after that to start a family." His transitions were more consciously planned than those of Miro, both towards employment and parenthood. At the age of 24 Simon moved in with his partner who was also a social worker in the same place and they rented a small flat in the city. They married after four years and had a child one year after that. Simon talked about fatherhood in terms of 'responsibility' in the same way as Miro. I think that everyone should walk along this road [parenthood] but that he has to be ready, has to have become responsible. Becoming a parent is a huge responsibility.'

While the decision to become a father was described by Simon as consciously taken and "at the right time", the decision that his wife should take up all of the parental leave was described by Simon as something not "discussed and decided" and "natural" in the same way described by Miro. Becoming a father affected Simon profoundly, in his words, making his life more satisfactory.

Parenthood also changed their housing situation. As a young co-habiting couple they lived independently in a rented flat. After marriage they decided to live with Simon's parents in their flat in order to save money to buy a flat, but soon after that his elder brother returned from England and the "flat became congested". Before their child was born they moved to his in-laws' house. Like Miro, Simon explained this in terms of the high costs of electricity and water to care for a child. Living with his in-laws also meant that he was not doing much housework. The expectation was that when his wife went back to her job after two years of parental leave they would live independently and buy or at least rent a flat.

Comparing the two Bulgarian examples Simon can be described as a career-oriented, work-focused father less involved in fatherhood and family life. His interpretation of the fathering role is more traditional in terms of breadwinning and only 'helping' his wife with childcare while she did other domestic tasks. Miro, on the other hand, was a child-oriented father reducing his work commitments in order to be more involved in childcare. He made a choice to move to a low-paid job with regular working hours in order to spend more time with his family. Miro, as a low-qualified employee, reconciled his low expectations about his work with an active caring identity, modifying to an extent the dominant cultural expectations of fathers. In our study he represents a 'transformative model of fatherhood' while Simon developed a strong professional identity negotiating a more traditional fatherhood role. Miro was learning to be a parent with few financial resources and limited life experience but felt proud of being actively involved in bringing up his children.[9] Simon made fewer changes in his work and followed a traditional path. Miro was closer to the Swedish father in acquiring 'gender competence' (Stauber, 2006), understood as a subjective awareness of gendered role models and making efforts to oppose the dominant gendered division of labour.

The Bulgarian examples illustrate young parents' high dependence on the extended family. Neither of the two fathers managed to gain sufficient economic capital through waged work before parenthood and had to rely on financial support from their parents. Having lived independently for a period before marriage, they moved to live with their parents or in-laws in order to share household expenses. In Bulgaria, raising a child has in many instances become a project of the extended family that provides money, childcare, housing and emotional support (Biggart and Walther, 2006). As elsewhere in Eastern Europe, in Bulgaria support from parents becomes even more crucial when young adults become parents and have their own children (Roberts, 2009.

Embedded in complex webs of relationships that provide support of various types, these young fathers' stories demonstrate how the different layers of context are important for understanding the biographical accounts about this phase in their lives. The shift from state-owned capital and generous state support to privatisation and cuts in state services have underlined the importance of the wider family network for the current generation of young Bulgarian parents. Even so, parents deployed agency in responding to the structural constraints of the labour market and coping with the uncertainty of the 21st century.

Comparing the transition to fatherhood across countries

The fathers in this chapter were selected to represent cases of working parents in countries with different institutional arrangements – a Northern European welfare state, an Eastern European post-communist country and a Southern European country (see Chapter Two). Like the analysis of working mothers in Chapter Four, the trajectories reveal both linear and non-linear patterns related to different layers of contexts and individual gendered life stories.

We have examined and compared the *timing* of the transition to fatherhood in relation to life course transitions during youth and early adulthood. Several patterns can be identified and demonstrate how the transitions between different life course phases affect fatherhood experiences and practices. In some of the life stories a more obviously linear pattern emerges as regards how the interviewees manage transitions, while in others non-linearity is prevalent and deviation from age-graded patterns are more frequent. This variation seems to mirror social class variation, with working-class men in Sweden and Portugal having linear trajectories into fatherhood. In these cases, the transition to fatherhood is often unplanned, something that "just happened". On the other hand, middle-class fathers have more non-linear trajectories as they, after leaving upper secondary school, often take gap years, spending periods of time exploring different types of work and leisure activities. Parenthood is "put on hold" in favour of temporary low-skilled jobs, different forms of education and travelling abroad in pursuit of challenging experiences. Not until they have created "the right circumstances", found "the right partner", established a stable economy and preferably found proper housing are they prepared to have a child. This means that the transition to fatherhood is often well planned but comes later in life for these men.

It is striking that the transition to fatherhood takes place, is looked on, and talked about in different ways depending on social class and educational background, but with some commonalities across countries. The three low-educated men, Linus, Miro and João, say that the transition to fatherhood "just happened". To be a father was part of their identity as men, and something they expected to happen. The higher educated men talk more in terms of planning fatherhood in relation to other strategic decisions. Paul, with a non-linear trajectory, talked about exploring and taking advantage of the different options available in a Swedish context but also following his religious beliefs. Irrespective of social class background, it appears that the transition to fatherhood was also much more a matter of concern for the *extended family* in Bulgaria and Portugal than in Sweden. Many young people in Bulgaria and Portugal do not move out of the parental home until they get married or have children, usually at the age of 25 to 30. In Sweden, most young adults move out at around the age of 19. For several of the Portuguese and Bulgarian interviewees in this study the housing situation made it necessary to live with their parents or parents-in-law after they had had a child. One of them, João, even moved back to his parents after he became a lone parent. The same pattern was observed among the mothers in Chapter Four. Living in an extended family opens up a range of advantages: not only are there better opportunities for handling financial strains, but there are also possibilities for childcare support, and practical and emotional support is close at hand. The possibility to combine work and family also increases when two generations take active part in childcare. The lack of parental support in everyday life was often discussed as a problem among the Swedish fathers as they only had a few people they could turn to when they needed childcare. Their own parents lived far away or had busy lives themselves.

However, living in an extended family can also have negative consequences, not least for gender equality as women traditionally have the main responsibility for domestic chores and childcare. In cases of close relationships between the generations, women relatives often bear the brunt of care. In this way the traditional gendered patterns are rarely challenged. Previous studies of fathers' participation in childcare have shown that in cases where men are required to take sole responsibility, gender equality increases. For example, Brayfield (1995) found that fathers take a more equal responsibility for the childcare when their partners work full time or at irregular times.

Welfare state context, and not least socioeconomic circumstances and *material resources*, strongly influence young people's life courses. For example, for many young adults in Bulgaria life after compulsory or upper secondary schooling is characterised by a struggle against rising expenses and the threat of poverty, demanding a clear focus on finding a job and earning money. Young low-skilled people from working-class backgrounds especially are often obliged to enter the labour market early in life to support themselves, this in a context of high unemployment rates, unsecure employment and low wages. Thus the lives of these men are characterised by insecurity. For those who have a more stable economic situation life is less insecure and trajectories more predictable. The life story of Simon is a typical example of this.

He had a linear educational trajectory and was eager to secure a stable family economy before he decided to have a child.

A privileged background and higher education matched with greater job opportunities and social security in Sweden allow young men to try out different jobs and to travel before settling down in professional occupations. This is in contrast to the poorer economies of Eastern Europe where the more privileged young men have a direct transition to the labour market and can follow the normative sequence of getting a job, partnership and fatherhood. Those from poorer backgrounds and with lower education face difficulties in establishing themselves in the labour market and oscillate between unemployment and precarious jobs. The case of Miro in Bulgaria also confirms this conclusion. Although he became a father early in life he was still unable to provide an adequate income for his family.

This analysis demonstrates that social class, level of education and income are among the important aspects affecting the transition to fatherhood. However, other dimensions such as family support can also make the impact of material circumstances different across contexts.

Notes

[1] See Lewis et al (2009) for a discussion of this topic based on data from the Transitions project.

[2] These are the main preferences also supported among the population (ISSP, 1998).

[3] In Sweden this means two years of education at university.

[4] This choice is associated with social class, as middle and upper-class students at that time (1986) qualified for university studies while working-class students chose a two-year programme that did not qualify for access to higher education.

[5] The university system has no tuition fees but it is very competitive to gain access. The state provides well-developed study loan schemes.

[6] This demonstrates the methodological point made in the Introduction, that caution must be excercised in the use of typologies across different studies.

[7] See Chapter Six for details of leave schemes across the countries at the time of the interviews.

[8] Student loans were only introduced in the country in 2005.

[9] See Brannen and Nilsen (2006) for discussions of similar cases of low-skilled fathers and their role as carers, describing a shift in fathers' roles from 'fatherhood' to 'fathering'.

SIX

Supports and constraints for parents: a gendered cross-national perspective

Janet Smithson, Suzan Lewis, Siyka Kovacheva, Laura den Dulk, Bram Peper and Anneke van Doorne-Huiskes

Introduction

This chapter considers the range of resources available for working parents in different national contexts. We draw on material from countries with different levels of public and private support, working hours and childcare, to provide a systematic overview and some cross-national comparisons of types and sources of constraint and support for working parents. Unlike Chapters Four and Five and the following chapter, the analysis is not based on the case studies of individual parents. Rather we conceptualise differences across countries with reference to the *structural characteristics* that provide support or constraints – the resources that can be drawn on to make working parenthood possible. Thus we analyse what the national contexts are 'cases of', where support for working parents is concerned. We have categorised sources and levels of support (see Table 6.1). We have also distinguished between three main types of support within these levels – regulatory, practical and relational (support from relationships within a workplace). Countries are first examined and categorised according to some of the key categories and comparators which were relevant to our research questions (see Tables 6.2 and 6.3) and which is in line with our multilayered case study approach (see Chapter Three), notably, formal state supports, organisational supports (policies, culture, managers and colleagues), childcare support, support from partners and wider family support. All of these are considered below, and we explore the links to gendered and cultural assumptions.

A cross-national comparative perspective delineates the social structural context of people's lives – in this study, public policy provision, workplace support and community and family support available. Whether this is identified by respondents as being of value to them in their everyday lives is, however, another matter. We therefore also take into account the kinds of support and constraints respondents take as given or fail to mention – what goes unsaid or is not viewed as important or relevant, and what is seen as an entitlement in each country.

Formal support from the state in the form of regulations and laws

Formal state support is greater in the Scandinavian and Eastern European countries than elsewhere. Employers in these countries are bound by regulations laid down by the state to implement lengthy paid parental leave, and in Sweden and Norway in this study, to provide flexible working hours during the period of breastfeeding. In the other countries such as the UK the state is less generous and seeks to persuade employers to act in a family-friendly way to employees, for example, by promoting a 'business case' in the UK, and increasingly so in the Netherlands. Employment protection is in general stronger in the Scandinavian countries than elsewhere. In the former Eastern bloc countries the right to lengthy paid parental leave is still in place and hence more generous than in many Western European countries, while other supports such as access to subsidised housing has radically diminished.

Table 6.1: Sources of support

Formal support			Informal support
Macro **National laws and** **regulations**	**Meso** **Organisation**		**Micro**
	Organisational **regulations**	**Organisational** **culture**	
Working time regulations	Organisational working time regulations	Managers and supervisors	Partner
Formal childcare facilities	Organisational childcare facilities and support	Colleagues	Wider family – grandparents, siblings
Leave regulations	Organisational leave policies		Friends and neighbours

Table 6.2: Organisation of time, leave and childcare: dominant model at time of study (2003-05)

Organisation of:	Bulgaria	Slovenia	UK	Netherlands	Sweden	Norway	Portugal
Working time norms	Full-time jobs for both partners	Full-time jobs for both partners	Part-time work for mothers, long working hours for fathers	Part-time work for mothers and full-time work for fathers	Over half (56%) of mothers with young children work full time. Nearly all fathers work full time	Over half (54%) of mothers work full time. Nearly all fathers work full time	Full-time jobs for both partners
Parental leave	19 weeks paid maternity leave, 21 months basic rate paid parental leave	15 weeks paid maternity leave, 90 days paid paternity leave, 260 days full paid parental leave	Six months paid maternity leave, six months unpaid, two weeks paid paternity leave, 13 weeks unpaid parental leave	16 weeks paid maternity leave and 13 weeks unpaid parental leave per parent with a child under eight	Eight weeks paid maternity leave, eight weeks paid paternity leave. Parents share 480 days of paid paternity leave per child	52 weeks paid maternity leave, four weeks paid paternity leave, 39 weeks paid parental leave, one year unpaid parental leave	16 weeks paid maternity leave, four weeks paid paternity leave, three months unpaid parental leave
Leave for caring for a sick child	Fully paid 60 days per year	14 days paid leave	None specified	10 days paid leave per year	120 days paid leave child/year	10 days paid leave per year	30 days per year (paid at 60%)

Table 6.2: continued

Organisation of:	Bulgaria	Slovenia	UK	Netherlands	Sweden	Norway	Portugal
Childcare	Mother's care in the home up to two or three years, then public childcare, supplemented by informal care from extended family	Mother's care in the home up to two or three years, then public childcare	Private nursery or childminder up to three, then state-funded nursery school part time for a year	Tripartite childcare system: parents, government and employers share the cost of childcare	Most children start public or private day care at 18 months. All childcare is subsided by the state and at low taxes	Cash for care scheme for under-threes (65%). In 2003 42% in nurseries	Mother's care up to five/six months, then informal family or paid care until three years and childcare (mostly private but state-supported) from three to five years
Age of starting school	School starts at seven, obligatory kindergarten at six	Six years	Four-and-a-half years	Four years	Six years	Six years	Six years
Hours of school per day in early school years	Four to five hours a day. After-school care is organised only at some schools and is paid by parents	Eight hours a day including free afternoon activities	Six hours a day. After-school care is provided by childminders, relatives or limited places in after-school care	Between three, five or six hours a day. Limited availability of formal after-school care	Depending on age, between three to seven hours	Three to four hours a day. Private after-school care	Six hours a day

Organisational support

State and workplace support are interrelated in many ways. Where state entitlements are lowest, some employers introduce work–family policies such as flexible working arrangements or family leave beyond the statutory minimum, on a voluntary basis, usually for business reasons. Parents may feel less sense of entitlement to take up such policies than in countries where these are legally mandated (Lewis and Smithson, 2001). On the other hand, even when there are statutory entitlements to, for example, generous parental leave or part-time work, these have to be implemented at the workplace level where organisational culture, informal practices, manager attitudes and colleague relationships, as well as global competition and associated management techniques, can all have an impact on the resources and supports available to parents (Lewis et al, 2009). In Bulgaria and Slovenia, the rising insecurity of jobs with diminishing state protection makes parents reluctant to use the statutory provisions to the full. There is often an implementation gap between policy (whether state or organisational) and actual practice, even in 'family-friendly' workplaces (Callan, 2007; Holt and Lewis, 2012).

There is evidence of gendered assumptions: conflating job commitment with hegemonic masculinity (Bailyn, 2006), and constructing ideal workers as those who do not allow work to interfere with family in all the countries, particularly in the private sector (Brandth and Kvande, 2002; Haas and Hwang, 2007). Besides gender, differences in job status also made a difference in the use of family-friendly workplace policies. In countries with liberal and conservative welfare states such as the UK or the Netherlands and Germany, high-status employees, especially in the private sector, had greater access to flexible working hours, for example, than front desk workers. In Bulgaria low-status workers used the lengthy parental leave and care leave for a sick child more often than high-status employees. The low-paid employees in low-qualified jobs did not lose much income during the long leave and would not gain as much career growth if they stayed in the workplace. The high-status workers usually cut some part of their legally allowed leave in order to demonstrate work commitment and to manage to keep up with the rapid changes in the job demands. Nevertheless, in all the countries parents talked about the important role that managers played in the everyday life of parents (das Dores Guerreiro et al, 2004; den Dulk et al, 2012), either in terms of exercising legitimate discretion or in informally providing or withholding support.

Statutory provision as well as formal organisational policies often include an element of line managers´ discretion. This is particularly the case in the Netherlands and the UK, where several statutory provisions explicitly include an element of discretion. For instance, while parents are entitled to flexible or part-time work in the two Scandinavian countries, both the Dutch and British managers can decline a request to reduce working hours when this is viewed as conflicting with serious business needs. The 'right to request' flexible working arrangements is particularly limited by managerial discretion in the UK (Fagan and Walthery, 2011 ; Fagan et al, 2006).

Relational support at work, from managers and colleagues, is a crucial resource for managing work and parenting (Olliere-Malaterre, 2010). Dynamic processes based in relations between social actors shape experiences and behaviours and are a crucial aspect of workplace context. Many of the parents talked about what can be termed a 'management lottery' (Brannen, 2009; den Dulk et al, 2012), suggesting an element of luck in the support received. Even in countries with more formally enshrined rights, a parent-friendly manager is very important for parents with young children and can be a source of both practical and relational support in certain situations or can undermine regulations in others. Managerial support varied both across and within organisations, often reflecting shifting contexts. In Bulgaria and Slovenia, with inflexible working time regulations, the role of managers is crucial in family emergencies (Kovacheva, 2009). In the private sector in Bulgaria new-style managers are described as those who are younger and schooled in capitalism, who regard support for parents as an unaffordable cost in a competitive environment. Old-style managers are more likely to provide informal support. In contrast, in the UK private sector company, new-style managers are described as those who are more likely to endorse informal support and flexibility while old-style managers endorse the traditional ideal worker ideology and expect constant availability. Elsewhere trends such as high commitment management stress the need to support employees' work–family needs to gain their commitment.

Colleagues provide another important source of relational support in the workplace. Where people work interdependently, especially in self-managing teams, such as in the Swedish social services, colleagues can become important for organising the working day in a flexible way. Colleagues cover for each other and such reciprocity is especially valued by parents of young children (Plantin and Bäck-Wiklund, 2009). However, this also has a downside. A common finding across the countries was that although colleagues could be important sources of support, parents were often reluctant to take time off when needed precisely because they knew that their colleagues would cover for them.

Thus colleagues' support was double-edged. This was due to intense workloads which meant that colleagues were already overburdened. This intensification of work was reported in every country as organisations strove to compete in the global economy or to increase efficiency (see Lewis et al, 2009). This, too, undermined to some extent supportive state or workplace policies.

Finally, as discussed in Chapter Three, we selected both public (social services) and private sector (finance) organisations because type of sector can affect employees' experiences of work. Public sector organisations did emerge as somewhat more supportive than the private sector in most cases in this study. However, this difference was declining with the prevalence of new public management (Christensen and Lægreid, 2007 whereby the public sector organisations adopted more market-oriented approaches, including cost-cutting and efficiency measures (Lewis et al, 2009). This generated the intensification of work which was characteristic of both sectors. For example, managers in the Swedish and Norwegian social services were happy to grant leave or part-time work but were often unable to replace the work that was relinquished, leading to intensification of work for the parent on leave or working flexibly, or for colleagues who must pick up the slack. In Bulgaria the private sector, especially the new small companies created with the transition to the market economy, did not always comply with statutory parental leave regulation. This happened in a context of diminishing state control and weakened trades union protection.

Childcare

Childcare facilities have been singled out as a separate source of support for several reasons, not least because affordable childcare is one of the most important resources for working parents. Their sheer existence is important in its own right. Such *practical* help offers parents the opportunity to work but is also reassuring, helping parents to feel secure that their children are being looked after in a safe place.

In Bulgaria parents consider subsidised childcare as their right. In villages with falling birth rates many kindergartens closed and working parents had fallen back on informal support from the extended family and neighbours. The ESS fourth wave (carried out in 2009) showed that Bulgarian parents still had the highest expectations of European parents about the role of the state for supporting working parents, despite parents' low levels of satisfaction with support for work–family balance and childcare (Kovacheva, 2010). In the Netherlands, in contrast, care at home by parents (the mother) was highly valued and considered best for the child, and childcare was usually used on a part-time basis. Too many hours in formal childcare was not considered good for the wellbeing of the child. Many Dutch parents considered three days as a maximum.

Support from partners

In terms of informal sources of support, the partners of working parents were very important in most instances both for *emotional* and *practical* support. However, on the practical side, different gender role ideologies across the countries affected the division of labour in the household between fathers and mothers. Participants did not usually define themselves explicitly in terms of gendered breadwinner/carer roles. Nevertheless their accounts of their working patterns and promotion opportunities reflected assumptions of male breadwinner/female homemaker orientations (Crompton, 1999), although participants did not use these terms. Norwegian and Swedish parents often aspired to shared parenting, although in these countries (among the most 'equal' in the world), women still did more of the domestic work and childcare than men. Scandinavian women were also more likely to report dissatisfaction with a male partner's involvement. Portuguese and Bulgarian women were least likely to express dissatisfaction, despite the low levels of paternal involvement in childcare and housework in those countries. Mothers' expectations of practical and emotional partner support were strongly influenced by gender role ideologies that affect intra-household negotiations. In Portugal and Bulgaria, there was an expectation that grandparents, especially grandmothers, helped a great deal with childcare, but not that the children's fathers would help substantially, and this affected how the mothers and fathers in these countries talked about their support, or lack of support.

In the second half of the 20th century the one party regimes in Eastern Europe established a pattern of gender relations in which both partners worked full time, supported by both state and enterprise welfare structures (Pascall and Kwak, 2005). The high rates of participation in full-time employment by women and men were, however, accompanied by a vertical and horizontal segregation, a significant pay gap and unequal division of unpaid domestic and childcare work (Stoilova, 2001; Mrcela, 2008). The social transition to a market economy and party pluralism after 1989 involved changes in the relationship between the state, the market and the family as main providers of services. In Bulgaria (to a lesser extent in Slovenia) explicit gender stereotyping resurfaced (Kovacheva, 2000). With the expansion of the paid part of parental leave and continued protection of mothers against dismissal, younger women in particular were increasingly considered unreliable workers, especially in private sector companies. Despite gender equality legislation in Slovenia, parenthood continues to be seen as a mother's responsibility. Younger women are often discriminated against in terms of jobs and promotions because they are viewed as potential mothers (Mrcela, 2008, p 153).

Wider family supports

When both partners were employed and where little formal childcare support was available, other informal sources such as the wider family, particularly grandparents, became important. Family support featured more typically in the interviews from Slovenia, Bulgaria and Portugal. However, it was also an important support for many of the UK and Dutch parents and, in some instances, a resource for working-class parents in the Scandinavian countries. In Slovenia and Bulgaria both family support and state support were important for childcare. Family support came to compensate for the inflexibility of public childcare and was an invaluable resource when parents worked extra hours, travelled on business trips or were involved in training and education.

In Northern Europe there was a strong discourse of autonomy and independence. However, the extended financial support often provided by parents in these countries to cover higher education and house buying were not viewed as dependency. This demonstrates, as with gendered expectations of partners, how perceived support and constraints can be viewed differently depending on the norms in a particular country. In the Netherlands, informal support by grandparents or childminders was widely used, although formal support existed.

Cross-national comparisons

In order to illustrate in more depth the differences between countries on these dimensions we have chosen to provide a description of selected countries from the study – Slovenia, the Netherlands, Sweden and Portugal, following the logic of the North/South/East divisions of European history (see Chapter Two). We focus on two of the main formal sources of support and constraint as perceived by working parents: affordable childcare and choice and flexibility of working hours, and view these in relation to informal support networks.

In most of the countries in this study, working hours were seen as critical. The Northern countries in this study all had high rates of part-time working, especially among mothers of young children (see Table 6.3). Where a workplace allowed flexible working hours this was often seen as a huge advantage by parents. In the majority of cases mothers, but not fathers, of young children reduced their working hours when this option was available. However, not all had the opportunity or the means to do so and then other resources had to be drawn on in order to make working parenthood possible.

Table 6.3: Employment rate in partner countries, 2003 (%)

Country	Total employment rate	Women in employment	Women in part-time employment
Bulgaria	52.5	49.0	1.1
Netherlands	73.5	65.8	48.7
Norway	75.5	72.6	32.5
Portugal	68.1	61.4	8.6
Slovenia	62.6	57.6	3.9
Sweden	72.9	71.5	25.0
United Kingdom	71.8	65.3	28.3

Note: Total employment rate in the age group 15-64.

Source: Eurostat (2004)

Part-time work and childcare – a 'private matter': the Netherlands

As Table 6.3 shows, the Netherlands had the highest rate of women working part time. The Dutch case is noteworthy in that there is a traditional division of labour between men and women and the idea of institutional childcare facilities has yet to be fully integrated into the Dutch system and mindset. Parenthood and childcare have been historically regarded as a private matter in this country. Only in the last decade of the previous century has childcare facilities entered the public discourse as a public concern. The high part-time rate among working mothers must be seen in the light of the ideological notion that children are best cared for by their mothers at home. Even in couples where the mother earns a higher income than the father, the mother in most cases reduces her working hours to care for the child. One Dutch mother, Nadine, who works in the private sector, explained her decision to reduce her hours, by referring to the fear of her partner losing his career perspectives when working part time and her own wish to spend more time with her child. This specific situation of Nadine indicates in a broader sense that the norm of motherhood is still strongly embedded in Dutch culture. This norm implies that at least part of the daily care of children needs to be provided by the parents themselves, preferably by the mother.

Employees (mainly mothers) are entitled to reduced working hours, and this is mentioned as one of the most important sources of support for parents in the Netherlands. However, as other studies demonstrate, part-time work can also be regarded as a constraint, limiting positive career development for women[1]. In the Dutch case part-time work was viewed favourably by interviewees. Part-time work was not presented as a gendered measure and it was not a right for mothers in particular. By law[2] Dutch employers are obliged to treat employees equally regardless of working time, and the Act on the Adjustment adjustment of working hours entitles all workers to reduce or extend working hours. Employers have to grant a request unless they can show that it conflicts with serious business needs (den Dulk et al, 2012). In a context of a traditional division of labour between men and women in the household, however, the majority of those who work part time are mothers.[3] The tacit trade-off that Dutch women accept is that part-time work entails no or very slow career progress.

Partner support is itself likely to be shaped by mothers' working patterns – part-time working gives mothers more time to spend with children and to take care of domestic tasks. The men in such households are hence the main breadwinners (where they work full time). Part-time working mothers are also a source of both practical emotional support for full-time working fathers, while full-time working husbands provide financial support and reassurance for mothers but at the expense of mothers' work careers. The situation of one Dutch couple illustrates this point. Gerben is a full-time working father and his partner, Nienke, is a part-time working mother. Gerben tried to fulfil his professional duties in four days a week. It often happened, however, that Gerben felt he had to go to his work on his day off. When this happened, Nienke says: "That is a nuisance; then I have to organise ad hoc day care and I don't like that." When Gerben – as the main breadwinner – was called to his work, Nienke defined it as her responsibility to organise the conditions for Gerben to go to his work. This is an interesting example of gendered responsibilities, adopted by both partners in a taken-for-granted way.

In the context of the gendered division of labour in the home, the gender segregation in the labour market and the gender pay gap, most responsibility for weaving the strands of work and family together fall on women, perpetuating gender inequalities.

Part-time work and childcare – a 'public issue': Sweden

The right to work part time is also an issue in the Scandinavian context. Many mothers in the Swedish social services reduced their working hours when they had children. However, when a distinction between long and short part-time hours is made, it is clear that mothers with higher education tend to reduce their working time to long part-time hours (four days a week) compared with those who have lower education.

Sweden has by far the best publicly funded childcare programmes of the countries in this study, and 80 per cent of one- to five-year-olds are in pre-school. In recent years the focus has been on keeping public childcare affordable, and a maximum price has been set. This is considered one of the main sources of support for parents (Bäck-Wiklund and Plantin, 2005). Swedish childcare, in contrast to childcare in the Netherlands, is a public issue, and has been so for many years. Moreover, where the Dutch authorities have chosen a 'private–public' partnership in the funding of childcare institutions, involving employers in their efforts to provide for their particular employees, Sweden has continued to see this as a provision of the welfare state.

In this context, Swedish parents do not look to their employers for support. In the social services, where the Swedish organisational case study was conducted, the practical and relational support of colleagues proved important. This was because these workers were organised in self-managed teams. In order to enable flexibility during the working day, such as staying at home with a sick child or taking children to the doctor, colleagues negotiated the 'lost' work time with one another, thus making being a working parent easier. This informal support provided flexible working hours but also contributed to goodwill and high morale at work. There was nevertheless a downside to this as parents were often reluctant to stay away from work as they knew that their already overburdened colleagues would have to take over their work. So this system would work better if there were enough staff.

Parents who had moved to the city for work often did not have family living nearby. For those who did have extended family nearby, the most frequent type of support available from kin was babysitting, which made leisure time possible for the couples.

In spite of having a high score on the GEM index it is accepted that mothers do the bulk of domestic work and childcare, whereas mothers have to *negotiate* with fathers if they want to share the tasks. The division of labour in the household frequently became an issue of conflict between partners, as the case of Patricia illustrates. Patricia picked up the children from nursery. This affected her work since she was the only one in her team with young children. She reported many heated discussions with her partner about this. When the children were ill she was usually the one who had to take time off. Asked if her partner could do more, she said:

> 'Of course he could. I mean if I can stay home, he can do the same. But he is a better negotiator than me and he always makes it sound like his work is more important than mine and that he HAS to do certain things at work. And in the end he earns a lot more than me and that's also something that matters....'

This quote illustrates a frequently recurring theme across the countries: how gendered structures, including the pay gap, shape parenthood and make motherhood different from fatherhood both in everyday family life *and* in the workplace.

Full-time working hours and childcare – a public issue: Slovenia

Like Bulgaria, Slovenia has moved from having a plan economy to a market economy, resulting in a decline in public services. Full employment and public childcare facilities were taken for granted in the former Yugoslavia, of which Slovenia was a part. After the transition to a market economy the situation for working parents became more stressful.

The part-time employment rate in Slovenia is low (Fagnani et al, 2004), and most mothers work full time, after a year or more of maternity and parental leave. There is, however, a legacy from the old regime, namely affordable public childcare. All the parents in the Slovenian bank who were interviewed made use of it. Since the opening hours of day care centres in many cases did not coincide with the parents' working hours, additional support had to be found. Most of the interviewees would not be able to balance work and family were it not for additional support from their families, especially mothers and mothers-in-law (Černigoj Sadar and Kersnik, 2005, p 55). In one case (Nina), both her mother and her mother-in-law helped out by picking up the children from nursery and by sometimes cooking the evening meal for the family.

Despite widespread public childcare in Slovenia, there is a strong tradition of family networks to be relied on if needed. In these networks, female relatives give practical assistance on an everyday basis. The gender division of labour in the household follows the same standard pattern in Slovenia as elsewhere. However, increased availability of family help serves to let fathers off the hook, as we can see in Chapter Seven in the case of Janez. The unusual case of Marija is also illustrative in serving to underline what is seen as the desirable norm, at least from a male point of view. Marija is a financial analyst with a degree whose partner is a student. Currently Marija is the breadwinner while her partner stays at home with their young daughter. They share the housework between them, and Marija seems satisfied with the situation. However, her partner, who was also interviewed, says that if he was working he would work full time and she would probably either take time off work or work reduced hours if possible, thus suggesting the strength of the male breadwinner model in fathers' perceptions (Černigoj Sadar and Kersnik, 2005, p 54). While in the Northern countries' interviews there was a theme about part-time work simultaneously helping and de-privileging mothers, in Slovenia and Bulgaria the long parental leave and sick child leave (taken mostly by women) were seen as a support but also an obstacle to gender equality.

Full-time working hours and childcare – a family issue: Portugal

Only the UK surpassed Portugal in terms of long working hours at the time of this study. However, where British mothers typically worked part time when they had young children,[4] both Portuguese mothers and fathers worked full time. There is no tradition of part-time work in Portugal apart from some recent flexible working hours schemes related to family-friendly policies in the public sector,[5] and there are no specific policies for parents in the private sector (das Dores Guerreiro et al, 2005). In two-income families, the juggling of long working hours, the lack of fit between nursery opening hours and working hours, and short maternity leave is in most cases solved with a combination of formal and informal care, such as help from kin. Only when parents and parents-in-law live far away from young families, or are ill or too old and frail to be of much help, are they not relied on for support (das Dores Guerreiro et al, 2005).

Family support for childcare comes in different varieties. In Alexandra's case, for instance (see Chapter Four), her in-laws moved in with the family to look after the children. Her mother-in-law did all the domestic work, including the cooking. In Dália's case (see Chapters Four and Seven), her parents lived with the family when she was working in order to help with childcare. Sergio, a father in a higher status position in the private company, was the only one whose wife stayed at home to look after the children. They also had paid help in the house, and his father sometimes helped with childminding.

Support from partners is shaped by gendered practices in Portugal along the same lines as in the other countries. As reported in Chapter Four, Alexandra had support from her parents when the first child was born, and they also had paid help in the house. Her husband did not take much part in either childminding or housework. In only one Portuguese case (a worker in the private sector company) did a mother report that she and her partner shared the housework. Where mothers had access to wider family, in most cases their mothers or grandmothers, the father's lack of help in the house was rarely remarked on as a constraint. It could be argued that support from wider kin, or paid help, absolves fathers from sharing family work. It avoids conflict and makes life possible, but perpetuates gender inequities.

The main difference between Portugal and the Eastern European countries (Bulgaria and Slovenia) that also report considerable help from kin is their greater public childcare provision compared to Portugal and the long parental leave in Eastern Europe.

Conclusion

In this chapter we have considered the main sources of support and constraints for working parents, and what support is expected or taken for granted. We have demonstrated how different regimes of working hours and different forms of formal and informal childcare and systems of leave create complex webs of support for parents of young children across the seven countries. The cross-national variation in type of support is related to current and historical institutional frameworks and regimes of welfare in each country. These regimes encompass state provision and regulation (working hours, parental leave and public childcare), informal care from family networks and gender practices as they shape the contributions of both mothers and fathers in the household and in childcare. We have also made explicit the importance of the organisational context, not only the existence of formal policies, but also relational support and workplace culture and practices on parents' understandings and take-up of the support, and the constraints in those countries that have discretionary policies. The relative importance of public or private sector employment varies in the countries in the study, as does the difference between parents with high and low employment status, and between fathers and mothers. We have also highlighted how childcare is variously considered a private, a family or a public concern, in the different national contexts, and how resulting practices have an impact on working hours, feelings of entitlement to support and specifically gendered experiences of constraints or support.

Gendered complexities underpinning the ways that parents talk about support and constraints are also highlighted. The gendered nature of parenting is acknowledged in some countries, and taken for granted in others. Fathers and mothers typically talk about constraints in different ways and in practice mothers are more likely to compromise their careers for family reasons. The gendered expectations of new fathers and mothers, as well as gendered organisational expectations, vary in the countries studied, but in every country mothers are more likely than fathers to take up the policies available for leave or flexible working. Part-time working, where available, is also overwhelmingly undertaken by women that, while supporting the transition to parenthood, also reproduces gender inequalities in the home and the workplace.

It is notable that in those countries with more equal gender roles, there is not only a higher expectation from fathers and mothers that fathers will participate in childcare and domestic work, but there is also more conflict between couples on this issue. Raised expectations of gender equality appear to take a while to translate into the experience of gender equality within households, and this is not helped by gendered expectations from organisations (managers and colleagues), nor by gendered state provision in some countries. In other contexts where extended family support is available and often essential for both parents to work, this can reduce tensions but can also absolve fathers from the need to make more significant contributions, thus perpetuating gendered family practices.

To understand the ways in which these complex contexts, support and constraints play out in the day-to-day lives of parents we turn, in the next chapter, to look at how comparable mothers and fathers experience their lives in the present as they confront different time frames as working parents. We explore how combinations of resources and constraints are reflected in more positive or negative evaluations of mothers' and fathers' lives and feed into feelings of pressure and/or contentment with their lot.

Notes

[1] The Norwegian case study report discusses this in some detail based on the focus groups, and similar viewpoints were expressed in the individual interviews. In both private and public sector organisations women expressed concern that part-time jobs could make them seem less committed to work than employees in full-time jobs, and hence they were afraid to lose out on

promotion opportunities and salary rises. In the Dutch case this only discussed in relation to fathers and less so for mothers (viewed as a personal choice between care and work).

[2] Which is also EU law.

[3] Only a private sector organisation was studied in the Netherlands, but in the public sector there is a slight trend for more highly educated men to share parental leave with their partners, that is, both working less than full time in the early years (Gambles et al, 2006).

[4] The part-time rate for mothers in Britain is the same as for Norway, approximately 42 per cent.

[5] The so-called 'continuous working day' means a six-hour working day (das Dores Guerreiro et al, 2005).

SEVEN

Being a working parent in the present: case comparisons in time and place

Julia Brannen and Nevenka Sadar Cernigoj

> The wellbeing of working parents is generated by different mechanisms in different domains. At home it is the peace, patience and mutual understanding and support that bring about joy and a sense of fulfilment. In some cases the feeling of guilt for not having enough time for child and partner gives rise to discontent and unhappiness. At work it is the challenges of change, innovation and high responsibility that create a feeling of wellbeing for career oriented (high status workers).... For other (lower status workers) the limited autonomy, the insufficient resources, the imprudent regulations generate a feeling of helplessness and alienation. Kovacheva and Matev (2005, p. 14).

This description of the daily life of parents could have been written by any of the teams in the different countries and could refer to either public or private sector employees. In fact it was written by the team in Bulgaria, the poorest country in our study and one that is still suffering from the reversals and changes that took place from the early 1990s – the fall of the communist bloc and the arrival of private markets. A clue to its authorship lies in the words that end the quotation – '[parents'] feeling of helplessness and alienation'. However, as we shall see, this is not the case for all working parents interviewed in Bulgaria. As we shall show, parents' feelings of time pressure and wellbeing vary according to their particular circumstances and resources.

In this chapter we examine the particular resources available to comparable cases of mothers and fathers. We also employ a temporal lens – at the point in parents' lives when we interviewed them (2004) in which the present is informed by biography, but also by current contexts and orientations to the future. Here the focus is on the concurrent work–family 'fit' (Moen, 2011) rather than over the life course, as already discussed in Chapters Four and Five. A major underpinning perspective is time in the context of the increased simultaneity of events (Brose, 2004) in 'the world at reach' (Schutz and Luckmann, 1983), the ways in which parents' everyday time worlds overlap and rhythms blur in relation to different social domains, creating a need to synchronise often irreconcilable timetables (Brose, 2004, p 7) and time meanings and often resulting in a feeling of a constant state of busyness and multitasking (Hochschild, 1997; Brannen, 2005b).

There are several ways we addressed the experience of being a mother and a father in the interviews. We asked parents how they organised their daily lives and who took responsibility for childcare and domestic (household) work. We examined the sources of support parents drew on which enabled them to conduct their daily lives. We asked how they negotiated work–family boundaries; how they synchronised the different tempos and time schedules which they and family members lived by; and their preferences and strategies for connecting/keeping separate work and family life. In addition our focus was on their feelings of wellbeing in the context of competing demands on their time – how it felt to be a parent, a worker and a partner at that particular time.

In this chapter we have selected parents similar with respect to gender, age of child, occupation and type of organisation, and we compare how they fared and experienced their lives as working parents, in particular examining the different resources available and drawn on.

First, we compare four cases of mothers – those with the least resources who work in the lower echelons of the public sector in care work. An analysis of the experiences of those employed in low-status public sector jobs provides a base line for assessing how European parents manage parenthood. In focusing on the less advantaged it is an *a fortiori* test for assessing the conditions and experiences of parenting in different contexts. We selected mothers with young children employed as care workers in social services in Portugal, Bulgaria, Sweden and the UK, countries which represent the full spectrum of political and institutional contexts and welfare regimes in Europe. Second, in order to extend the analysis to fathers, we compare three cases of high-status fathers all employed in the private sector in similar occupations, again across a spectrum of countries, this time from Norway, Slovenia and the Netherlands. In both sets of cases we look at the domains of their lives and the resources available to them, how they act on and experience these domains and their responsibilities, with particular reference to time pressure and wellbeing.

Being a mother: low-status care workers across Europe

In Table 7.1 we set out briefly the current circumstances of the four mothers with respect to age of child, marital status, occupation, working hours, presence of parents nearby, childcare, housing, travel to work time, partner's work and help with childcare and domestic work. These mothers are working class according to their own and partners' occupations and background. In Chapter Four we showed how the transition to adulthood of many low-status workers was less protracted than among high-status workers since they moved from early school leaving or the completion of upper secondary level education straight into the labour market. Three of these women began their work careers in care work classed in all countries as low to medium-skilled work. Their partners were in similar level occupations. They vary, however, in terms of the age at which they became mothers, their housing histories, their current travel to work conditions, their kin networks and access to public affordable childcare and so on. We discuss each case in turn, comparing and contrasting cases in a cumulative way, in relation to their particular current experiences of and conditions for being a mother.

Table 7.1: Current circumstances of mothers in the study

Portugal *Dália, care worker, two-year-old child, husband is an unemployed carpenter*	Sweden *Susanne, care worker, two-year-old child, husband is a youth worker/ musician*	Bulgaria *Rosa, care worker, four-year-old child, husband is a driver in a local firm*	UK *Carol, care worker, two-year-old child, lone parent*
Works full time	Works part time (80%)	Works full time	Works full time
One hour travel to work per day	Three hours travel to work per day	Works locally	Travels by various means – one hour per day
Parents live in same city; now live in their house	Parents not nearby	Parents nearby	Only father lives nearby
Grandmother does childcare in child's home	Local public day care	Local public day care	Private nursery near workplace
Partner does little childcare or domestic work	Partner shares domestic work and childcare equally	Partner reported as supportive – does specialised tasks	Live-in partner does little childcare or domestic work

Dália (38), also described in Chapter Four, lives in Portugal and works as a care worker in social services located in an old part of Lisbon. Despite having some health problems around the birth of her first child (aged 30) she had a second child mainly, she says, for her son's sake. The birth of her second child was more difficult but her manager was supportive. Dália only took four months' parental leave, and says that her employer allows her to take the occasional day off for her children's illnesses. She also mentioned her entitlement to be exempt from working nights until her children were 13.

As shown in Chapter Four, a key to Dália's experience of her life is shaped by the support she receives from her parents, her mother in particular. Dália's husband has been unemployed for more than a year. On a working day Dália leaves the house at 6.30pm and drives to work for approximately half an hour, dropping off her father en route at his workplace. Her eight-year-old son goes to school on his own, while her mother looks after the younger child until Dália returns from work at 3.00pm, whereupon her mother goes to her own workplace. Because of her mother's availability Dália is able to work at weekends and does not have to plan her holidays. Despite being unemployed her husband does no housework or childcare except to "stay with the baby for an hour or two, now that she is a bit grown up". Dália does not appear to be critical of this: "Domestic work is for the women of the house." Her lack of criticism may be because she expects him to spend time looking for another job or that he is working in the grey economy while drawing unemployment benefit. Her very brief comments suggest that she was reluctant to talk about it.

Although Dália says her work was hard, she enjoyed her job and was able to concentrate without worrying about her children. When she was not at work, she describes taking her son to his activities, a further justification for working and for running a car as well as for her own commuting needs. Portuguese women invest strongly in motherhood, even more when their jobs are not intrinsically rewarding, and they use their income to provide for their children's needs and wants. Dália was happy to be able to get home mid-afternoon, allowing her some time to be with her children.

A key theme of her account relates to time and the difficulties of synchronicity (Brose, 2004) in reconciling the time schedules of the many domains that Dahlia and her family negotiate. The time schedules of being a mother and being a worker and transporting children and herself to their respective destinations mean that she found little time for herself. Yet Dália came across as relatively content with her lot, accepting the limitations and reporting no difficulties in separating her work and her family life: "I usually say that when I arrive at the office door, my family problems stay out and when I leave and pass the door again, my work problems stay here." This was made possible by considerable childcare support from her parents. The fact that the grandparents lived with the family during the working week and provided considerable practical help and also material help was critical to her sense of wellbeing. Material support was especially welcome as Dália's husband was unemployed.

Susanne (28) lives in Sweden and works as a care worker in a centre for those with mental problems, work that she enjoyed greatly. Typically most Swedes complete upper secondary level education but Susanne did not go on to further education. Aged 20, she wanted to get married (not so typical in Sweden) and to have children. The couple depended on public childcare for their son who started day care when he was one-and-a-half years old at the end of Susanne's long period of paid parental leave. Susanne and her husband shared parental leave, taking 16 months' leave between them, enabling them to be at home for as long as possible: "We were very poor during that time but it was worth it. That's why I could stay home for nine months and my husband seven months." This way of extending the parental leave is common among the Swedish interviewees who see themselves as "good parents" by postponing their children's start in day care.

Unlike Dália, Susanne was fortunate in having high quality, affordable public childcare that was available locally. But unlike Dália, they had no parents living close by to fall back on for support, such as when the child was ill and unable to go to day care. Moreover, the couple lived far from the city where Susanne worked, which added to the length of the working day. Having recently moved to their new house, they had few friends in the neighbourhood to help with babysitting, although they belonged to a local church.

On the other hand, under Swedish law Susanne was entitled to reduce her hours on her return to work to diminish time pressures on the family. Susanne worked four days a week, having a day off in the middle of the week, giving her a much needed break from commuting. Each working day Susanne had to leave home very early to get to her workplace where she started at 8.00am. She depended on her husband to take and collect their son from day care. Officially there is no official flexi-time in her centre and as her work involved contact with clients she was unable to work from home. However, her manager allowed her time off if she made it up later. She had been fortunate in negotiating a special arrangement whereby she could leave work 15 minutes earlier each day and arrive 30 minutes later than her colleagues *without* a reduction in her wages. This enabled her to catch trains without having to wait for long periods. Without this benefit Susanne's commuting time would be four hours a day instead of three.

Susanne enjoyed her work despite the long commute, feeling very committed to her colleagues and clients. Also like Dália, but unlike many workers, because of the nature of her frontline care work with clients (that takes place in a centre), Susanne placed clear boundaries around work, leaving it behind when she got home.

Susanne's welfare was sustained by the fact that her husband took full responsibility for taking and collecting their son to and from day care, which lessened the pressures on her. The couple shared the household work fairly, with Susanne conscious of how rare this was even among Swedish couples, and suggested that becoming a mother had improved her relationship with her partner. Susanne enjoyed motherhood and believed that it helped her empathise with her clients: "Yes … you turn into another person when you become a mother, it is inevitable. You feel more mature, and it spills over at work and even at home." But, like Dália, she put her child first. In order to manage competing time pressures, she "makes" time, creating "special times" to be with her son, her favourite time being when they sat together on the sofa watching children's television. Yet because of her long travelling time, Susanne still felt she lacked sufficient time to spend with him, and regretted putting him into day care at one-and-a-half-years old, something she had had to do because of their need for two salaries: "I didn't put him into day care because he needed it. It was more we who had to work."

Rosa (24), discussed in Chapter Four, lives in Bulgaria. She works in social services. Rosa had a great deal of help from her parents and parents-in-law after the baby was born and the couple lived with her in-laws to start with. The baby was fretful and Rosa felt very inexperienced. Rosa saw it as 'normal' for her to take the long leave while her husband devoted himself to earning the family income. Her husband and mother-in-law convinced her that returning full time (there were no part-time options and parents could not afford to take them up even if they were available) to her old job in social assistance at the end of maternity leave was the best strategy – it offered both security and very reasonable working hours. Public sector employment is seen as less risky by Bulgarian mothers, enabling them to take up the very substantial sick leave offered under law when their children are ill.

Rosa was additionally supported in being able to send her daughter, aged three, to the local public kindergarten: "I am very relaxed that she is in the kindergarten while I am here." When her daughter was ill (as she was quite frequently) Rosa was able to stay off work without problems. After a week away from work Rosa says she could depend on her mother-in-law to look after her daughter.

In many ways Rosa's case combines the good fortunes of both Dália in terms of kin support and of Susanne in terms of public (state) support. Like Dália, Rosa has considerable support from kin, but in Rosa's case from her husband's mother as well as from her own mother. Her ties with kin were strong, as is the case for many Bulgarians of this generation who have lived with their parents until marriage (and sometimes after marriage) and who often depend on help from kin to purchase housing – housing loans being very risky especially following the vagaries of the Bulgarian financial sector in the late 1990s. Like Susanne, Rosa also can depend on affordable local day care provided by the state for children aged three to seven, even though it is uniform and inflexible in terms of hours and days. She was also supported by two years' paid parental leave after her child's birth (135 days at 90 per cent of salary and the remaining two years at a flat rate).

Unlike Susanne's job, Rosa's job is more precarious, although public sector employment is less precarious than private sector employment in Bulgaria. In the context of considerable change and instability in recent years in Bulgaria, Rosa felt "lucky" to have a job. She also felt fortunate compared with many people she knew in having a healthy child, a supportive partner, generous parents on both sides as well as a secure job in the state sector.

The fact that the situation of Rosa and her family was on an 'even keel' meant that Rosa appeared relatively content. She described her husband as helpful, driving Rosa and their daughter to work and childcare in the mornings and evenings. Rosa was, however, the parent who took sick leave when the child was ill. Her workplace did not object when she took leave that helped Rosa to manage the asynchronicity between the time worlds of her workplace and that of small children.

In general Rosa found her workplace conducive – family matters flowed 'naturally' into work in the way they were discussed at work. Like Dália and Susanne, work did not impinge on Rosa's home life. Rosa had low expectations of promotion (there are few opportunities in low-skilled work), which in turn may have contributed to her wellbeing, encouraging her to take up the full amount of the extensive parental and sick leave for a child then available in Bulgaria. Being in the public sector also reduced her fear of job loss. In this context work could be enjoyed less for the nature of the work and more for the sociability it entailed. As Rosa notes: "Look at us here. We are all young mothers working here. I look forward to come here in the morning and enjoy laughing and talking with them." With the relaxed atmosphere at work and the considerable formal and informal support available to her, Rosa's account of her life did not sound time-pressured.

Carol (30) lives in London. She works in a centre run by social services for adults with learning disabilities. Carol grew up outside London and followed her mother into care work, first working alongside her in an old people's care home during the school holidays: "I've worked since I was 14. 'Cos we never had much money as a family, so we always tried to work." Carol left school at 16 with minimal qualifications. She met her child's father at the age of 20 and they went to London in search of better job prospects. But Carol soon returned to care work. She had a couple of spells of unemployment and short-term contracts, suggesting that care work was not necessarily secure even in a British context (where there is considerable demand for care workers). Carol had no plans to become a mother, a point that is significant for how she later felt about motherhood: "I just always assumed that we would always live together and get married and not have children and have a nice car each and a nice house [...] and holidays."

After the birth she took the available paid maternity leave of six months and was pleased to return to her full-time job as she did not bond well with the baby and felt lonely and isolated at home. Her partner was not supportive and within months their relationship broke down. Carol found working full time very hard going and managed to negotiate slightly shorter hours so that she could collect her child earlier from childcare. However, her manager soon pressed her to return to full-time hours by which time Carol was separated and having to manage on only her own income and so could not afford to work part time. Without a partner part-time work was not a possibility, especially as she had a large mortgage – Carol and her partner had taken out a loan based on their joint earnings just before the birth of their child. In fact Carol could not afford to pay the mortgage and they sold the house very quickly. Carol moved into a smaller extremely poor quality flat – "I have no heating and I have windows that are falling out" – in what she described as a 'rough area'. She applied for public housing, but was told she was low priority. She felt that she would be better off living as a lone mother on benefits, but her work was important to her.

Carol enjoyed her work. However, there was high staff turnover and the centre frequently had recourse to agency staff resulting in low morale and work overload. Carol had been there for eight years and in that time she had gained some qualifications (equivalent to upper secondary level schooling) and had taken a specialist course.

This suggests considerable commitment to social services and her occupation.

Her workplace was inflexible. If Carol needed time off for her son, she had to take annual leave and felt discriminated against compared with the managers: "Managers have children and they never explain themselves when they're off ... they are just off and it's fine." If she took time off she also felt guilty about the extra burden on her colleagues.

Even though Carol had a new partner at interview, she did not find family life any easier. Her account is suggestive of the experience of time acceleration (Rosa, 2009): she described the start of her working day as a rush to get her son ready for day care, resulting in conflict and stress. At work, although she enjoyed her job, she felt under constant pressure, often working through her lunch break. At the end of the day she depended on a colleague giving her a lift to the nursery or had to take the child and buggy on the bus or walk for half an hour – a long time in bad weather. Carol could not easily switch off from work when she got home. This was exacerbated by the fact she often had to do preparatory work in the evenings.

She felt she coped best in the evenings if she stuck to rigid time routines with her child that might make life even more stressful for herself. She had no support from her new partner and, as he was not the child's father, she considered it inappropriate to insist. While accepting his lack of parental responsibility, she was resentful he did not pull his weight in other ways, for example, by paying half the bills. In practice Carol felt she was a lone parent and while accepting the responsibility, found she could not enjoy and relax into motherhood as she felt she should. She often took out her frustration and anger on her partner and son, having outbursts of temper and periods of irritability. The fact that the couple worked in the same workplace was unlikely to help the situation.

Comparing mothers

In most domains Carol's experience of motherhood compares poorly with the experiences of Dália, Susanne and Rosa. In part this is because Carol had not wanted a child to start with, and found it difficult when the baby arrived. It is also to do with the break-up with her child's partner. Lone motherhood can be difficult without support. Carol's new partner did not alleviate the situation. In terms of availability of kin support, unlike Rosa and Dália, but like Susanne, Carol lacked close kin living in London except for her father who lived nearby and provided some support with childcare. Her husband's kin were no longer available after the couple split up. Unlike Rosa's parents, Carol's parents were unable to support her with housing in the context of her marriage break-up.

Carol's access to childcare was also more difficult than it was for the other three mothers. Unlike Rosa and Susanne, but like Dália, Carol could not rely on locally provided public childcare that she could afford. In part this was because Carol was living in a very big city but it was also because the UK has no infrastructure of public childcare for young children. Carol's housing situation was also particularly difficult, reflecting the 'London factor' of very high housing costs and little public housing. With no partner to share the mortgage, Carol's situation was worse than the other three mothers. Carol lacked a number of sources of support and found life difficult. She felt time-pressured and was very rigid about her son's routines and obsessive about housework. This did not encourage her new partner to be more involved. The fact that she was committed to her job was a strength but also a weakness, given that her workplace was marked by high turnover, low morale and work overload. While work made Carol feel better about herself and her life, it put too much pressure on her as a mother. Carol contrasts markedly with these three mothers in terms of her feelings about motherhood now and also the conditions for motherhood.

By contrast, Dália, Susanne and Rosa were largely content with their lot as mothers. Dália had a strong reason not to be content given her husband's unemployment and his failure to pull his weight with housework and childcare. But Dália was happy because of her parents' presence in the house, in particular her mother's help with caring for the two-year-old while Dália was at work, but also their financial help (they were both working). On a daily basis Dália could run a car, taking herself and her father to work while they lived in an area where it was possible for the eight-year-old to take himself to school. Susanne's life was logistically more complicated than Dália's in that the couple lived far from her workplace, requiring Susanne to make a long commute. Also on the negative side, the couple had no family living nearby or friends (yet) in the neighbourhood. Yet Susanne was more or less happy because she was able to have a day off mid-week. They also had a new house and there was locally available high quality public childcare. Still she felt she lacked time with their son. On the other hand, this negative feeling was offset by the fact that her partner was very involved in the child's care and shared the household work equally.

Similarly Rosa (from Bulgaria) seemed happy, perhaps a little more so than Dália in the Portuguese context. Even so, both had experienced material hardship. Rosa was acutely aware in the Bulgarian context of the difficulties of many people she knew in her community. By contrast with their lives, Rosa counted herself fortunate, at present at least, perhaps because of her low expectations. Indeed life was difficult for Rosa when she got pregnant. She was not married and had no job but was fortunate in being found a job through informal sources. Moreover, even though she was in the job for only a short time, Bulgarian law entitled her to three years' parental leave (two years paid at a low rate). Moreover, like Dália, she had considerable material help from parents (her own and her husband's). Furthermore, the state also provided, as it did for Susanne in Sweden, affordable public childcare that was available in her neighbourhood. In terms of their partners' help with childcare and domestic work, the picture is more variable. Only Susanne's husband pulled his weight (reflecting the public discourse of gender equality in Sweden), but the situation for Dália and Rosa was mitigated by plenty of help from kin.

All three mothers working in social services reported few problems at work or with taking time off if they needed to for their children (although all three had other back-up support). Only Susanne was able to work part time, but she was probably the only one who could afford to. All three felt able to leave their work behind them when they went home, reflecting the low status of their jobs and the bounded contexts in which they worked.

Five conditions emerge in these stories as important in enabling mothers to feel secure and content. They are: (a) a satisfactory housing situation; (b) a stable and relatively supportive relationship with the child's father (at least emotionally if not one involving an equitable sharing of responsibilities); (c) local, affordable institutional childcare; (d) substantial support from locally available extended family (parents); and (e) workplace support. Some of these conditions are underpinned by policies and practices at national and local levels, notably housing and childcare. Others are indirectly shaped by societal context. For example, Sweden is the only country among these four where gender equality is part of the public discourse. Intergenerational kin support is not legislated for but is a key component of parental support in each societal context. Kin support emerges as a key factor buttressing deficiencies in the other three conditions. As we have seen, in some contexts intergenerational kin support becomes more critical than in others.

None of the four mothers' situations meets all these conditions. With the exception of Carol, the other three mothers reported little difficulty in the workplace in terms of support for their care responsibilities. In terms of the other four conditions, Dália lacked a supportive partner and local affordable childcare but was compensated by having plenty of kin support. Susanne lacked kin support but was compensated by having the other conditions. Rosa's situation met all the conditions. By contrast, Carol experienced an unsupportive workplace environment, lived in unsatisfactory housing, was separated from the child's father and had a less than supportive current partner, had little affordable local childcare available to her, and lacked a local supportive kin network. Not surprisingly she was far from content.

However, time pressures and the issues of synchronising different timetables was a common theme across all four mothers' accounts. How they dealt with time pressures and asynchronicity depended on their different resources – material, relational and personal.

Being a father: high-status private sector workers across Europe

The decision to focus on high-status (rather than low-status) fathers in this chapter is partly a consequence of the choice of cases available.

Historically we may expect to find a less differentiated picture of fatherhood compared with motherhood (Brannen et al, 2004). *Fatherhood* is defined in institutional terms while *fathering* may be defined as active engagement in caring responsibilities (Brannen and Nilsen, 2006). In all European countries fathers expect to be full-time workers even where they are no longer sole breadwinners. Yet in most countries mothers still have the main responsibility for children, although active fatherhood is an official discourse in Scandinavian countries (Bäck-Wiklund and Plantin, 2005). Only in Scandinavian countries is there a statutory expectation that fathers be involved with their children at an early age. Norwegian fathers, for example, are entitled to one months' paid parental leave, the 'daddy quota', which is not transferable to the mother and hence is lost if they do not take it up. In other countries, at the time of the study, leave reserved for fathers was minimal, taken around the time of the birth (paternity leave) and usually unpaid (see Chapter Six).

In Table 7.2 we set out briefly the current circumstances of three fathers.

Bengt (31) is Norwegian. He is clearly a committed father but came across as rather burdened by the experience. His partner was his age and the couple had cohabited for six years; they had a two-year-old son. Both had university degrees. Bengt worked full time for a large multinational as a contracts consultant, while his partner was an administrator, also in the private sector. Bengt was unusual in having taken up half the parental leave; he took five months while his partner took seven months. Bengt belongs to the 13 per cent of Norwegian fathers who took more than the one-month quota. Both returned to work full time after parental leave. However, unlike his partner, Bengt felt punished for taking such long leave since his employer regarded his leave taking as evidence that he did not take his job sufficiently seriously. Bengt believed that he had not been given the salary increase due to him and felt he has been passed over for promotion within the company. If the couple has another child (a statistical likelihood), Bengt says that he would be more careful next time and would only take one month off; he would first negotiate with his boss that taking leave would not affect his career. Indeed, fathers who take out more than the paternity leave they are entitled to often meet difficulties in their organisations (Brandth and Kvande, 2002; Lewis and Cooper, 2005).

Table 7.2: Current circumstances of fathers

Norway	Slovenia	The Netherlands
Bengt, child aged two, high-status employee, multinational, wife is an administrator in the private sector (full time)	Janez, children aged 6 and 11, medium-status employee in finance, wife is in the public sector (full time)	Chris, seven-month-old baby, high-status employee in finance, wife is a high-status worker in IT
Works a five-day week	Works a five-day week	Works four long days
Grandparents not local	Grandparents local	Grandparents local
Childcare: public childcare	Childcare: wife and grandparents	Childcare: crèche and grandparents
Considerable gender equity	No gender equity	Some gender equity

Bengt's early involvement in his son's care is reflected in his use of flexible working available to all the employees in his company – Bengt used the opportunity to get to work early, sometimes around 7.00am. His partner had fixed hours and started later, at 8.00am, and took their child to day care. Bengt leaves work between 2.30pm and 4.00pm in order to pick up his son from the local public day care. They have dinner around 4.30pm. He says his partner cooks most of the time but Bengt reported "tidying up and doing the dishes". If the weather was okay he went outside to work in the garden with his son. Bengt often put his son to bed, usually at the child's request. This happened around 8.00pm; the couple went to bed around 10.00pm.

Bengt saw his life as time-pressured and stressful; in addition to his job and his involvement with his son, he was committed to finishing the decoration of their new house and was also studying to gain further qualifications. In answer to a question about the best times of day, Bengt mentioned interstitial or 'in between times': having lunch at work and seeing his son when he came home. He felt he did more than his partner at home and with their son; he complained that his son was too attached to him, blaming the long parental leave. While he enjoyed being with his son, he thought his partner should do more. Life for Bengt seemed "all work":

> 'Because as I see it I work from when I get up until I go to bed. At work, the garden, the house and all. In addition my son, he is following me. But she, she sits down and watches television, sleeps on the sofa and. I feel she has turned the traditional gender pattern upside-down....'

On the other hand, Bengt liked orderliness in the home: "I do not like if I find crumbs after the last person there. I am a meticulous perfectionist at that field, while she isn't."

Interestingly, despite the availability of public, affordable childcare in the neighbourhood, Bengt wanted to move closer to his parents who lived in a small city in the south west of Norway in order to get more help with their child. Bengt missed going out in the evening to enjoy himself. They had not felt able to ask the neighbours to babysit since their neighbours had their own families living nearby and did not need them to return the favour.

In short Bengt was ambivalent about fatherhood. He enjoyed the safety and predictability of life with his partner and child, but at the same time felt restless and afraid of leading a "boring life". He felt he only had time for work and family life. Although he enjoyed being with his son he resented it at the same time as it encroached on 'his time'. On the positive side, he was able to take lengthy parental leave and had flexible working hours, while on the negative side, he felt his career and salary affected by the former. He also had other time-demanding commitments (studying and doing up the house). Yet, rather than blaming the 'time squeeze' (Hochschild, 1997; Southerton 2003), he tended to blame his partner and saw the solution as needing more support which meant moving nearer to his own family.

Janez (35) is Slovenian. He came across as not very involved in fathering but was more or less content with life. He is a middle to high-status worker in the finance sector, married with two children aged 6 and 11, in his mid-thirties. Having finished secondary school where he specialised in computer sciences and completed military service he found work at 21 as a computer programmer in the private sector. He says he always expected to get married and have a family. After marriage, the couple moved to their own house and had a child, a natural and self-evident next step in life, from Janez' point of view. By the time he was 25, he "had it all" (his own expression): a job, a car, a wife, children and a house. Since then he saw his life as going along in the same vein. Janez and his wife worked full time, his wife in the public sector. Janez described preferring to keep his two worlds of work and family life separate.

Although not an involved father, Janez thought that family roles were in general becoming more equal. Fathers were no longer, in his view, merely authority figures. Janez' wife, together with her parents, were the main carers of their children. He justified his lesser involvement in terms of the children being "more attached to their mother". While he thought men should make an effort to be involved, mothers were seen as more important in satisfying children's needs: "It is a fact." He thought that fathers accepted this and "take the easiest way". Like other Slovenian fathers (and mothers) he accepted a gendered division in household work. This was explained not only in terms of fathers' lack of willingness to be involved but also in terms of the high standards women set by high housework standards and the strong emotional ties between mother and child, the latter, he says, making fathers' involvement difficult.

> 'Well it is a fact, no matter how much you are trying, the children are still more attached to the mother, at least as far as their needs are concerned. [A child] will never say: daddy give me something to eat ... well you may jump in but ... really you could only sit there and vegetate if you would want to ... if you want to be active ... you have to make an effort. But it is true that the majority of us are made to take the easiest way.'

Janez described fatherhood as 'challenging'. But he thought that, as the children grew older, parents needed to become more engaged, especially in the children's school activities. More important than fathers' roles in Slovenian family life was intergenerational help. As in Janez' family, grandparents also came to the rescue of their adult children, solving financial and housing problems, and providing childcare for their grandchildren and collecting them from kindergarten.

In short, Janez did not feel overburdened by fatherhood. He felt relaxed about playing a secondary, somewhat passive role currently, and expressed few negative feelings in his interview. He experienced little time pressure and was able to set clear boundaries around work and family. When he faced problems at work, he says he took time for himself and kept them away from his family. Thus he saw home as a haven and protected his family and himself from the burdens of outside problems, in particular trying to talk as little as possible about his job. He felt lucky to have intergenerational help.

Chris (33) lives in the Netherlands. He saw himself as an involved father although not as involved as his partner. The couple came from solid middle-class backgrounds and had a seven-month-old child. Chris was a high-status employee working in finance, just like his father before him. His wife studied law, just like her own father. His wife was similarly a high-status private sector employee but working in an IT company as a product manager. The couple had postponed becoming parents. However, at interview, Chris still felt he was pushed into fatherhood by his wife who felt she could not wait any longer to get pregnant (the 'biological clock' phenomenon). By then Chris was already well established in his career, having worked for the company for seven years.

In the same year that the baby was born, the couple moved to the outskirts of a city to a child-friendly neighbourhood. The move out of the city centre where they had previously lived was considered an important condition for having a child. Their house in city centre was "just no place for kids", even though Chris and his wife really loved it: "It was awfully nice; we lived in Utrecht centre on a canal, really downtown." At the time of the interview Chris's main concern was the renovation of the new house.

The couple had synchronised their working time schedules to accommodate what they saw as a good way of balancing their son's time – with more time at home and less time in institutional care. At the time of interview Chris worked full time – 36 hours a week – and had the option of different kinds of flexible working arrangements. Chris chose his compressed working week – a four-day week involving long days of nine hours each – following the birth, although the justification he gave for this is a bit ambiguous in that he only mentioned first the 'luxury' of extended time away from work before the benefits for childcare: "I chose Wednesday, jolly good: two days on, one day off, two days on and then the weekend. This is really inconceivable luxury, and you are just one day with the little one." By contrast his wife found it difficult to return to work having taken four months' paid leave; she says her manager and colleagues were not helpful. She too worked four days a week, slightly fewer hours than Chris – 32 hours a week as she was taking one day of parental leave. She planned to move to another job as she felt insecure, mainly due to a reorganisation while she was on leave.

Chris and his wife looked after their child one day a week each. The child was taken by Chris's wife to a private crèche near her workplace two days each week. Chris's mother looked after the child one day a week. The couple were happy with the arrangement as it limited the time their son spent in the crèche: "that is busy enough for him". Usually one set of grandparents stepped in if the child was ill.

Chris and his partner had not discussed the division of labour in respect of their son's care but assumed they would both continue working after the birth. Chris never envisaged doing a great deal of the childcare and was now surprised how much he enjoyed it. His wife did most of the caring when she was around – she got home first – and Chris was happy with this: "… in my view there should not be room for two captains on one ship, constantly quarrelling what is better and what should be done in what order; I just follow her in that, so to say. I do a lot myself, but she does evidently more. Partly because she is more likely to worry, to be concerned, to realise when he wants something, I just walk in the way or I put him in his play pen." The time squeeze appeared to be more of an issue for his wife than for Chris. Although Chris says he did as much of the household chores as his wife, his wife would like hired domestic help to give her more time.

However, despite the flexible working often, Chris experienced time pressures at work – he had no time to stay late at the office: "No, I just don't have time for that. Look, before we worked later and came home later.... I absolutely do not do this anymore, not intentionally, sometimes it is even very difficult to put down the work, just because you know there is a lot burning at your desk."

On return from his long days at work, Chris appeared to get off childcare lightly, reporting that his partner had fed and bathed their son by the time he got home. His evenings were relaxed while for his wife they were 'somewhat busier'; she reported in her interview the need to get everything ready for the next day. Chris says: "I usually slouch around and watch telly." Reflecting the traditional character of father involvement, he engaged in play: "We laugh and romp a bit." However, he was in sole charge of his son one day a week. Significantly, unlike his wife, he never worried about their son when he was at work. Chris enjoyed parenthood, the reason for this becoming apparent as he talked, namely his low expectations for enjoying being a father of a young baby: "It is inconceivably nice. Even now … I cannot do much with him [seven months old]. He does not understand anything yet. He is terrifically dependent on me and of course there is not much in return. We cannot play football yet. But it is nice already now! *I had not expected that."*

On the other hand, Chris was busy with the renovation of the house, leaving him little time, he says, for himself or for friends. The couple spent little time just being together. He saw having a young baby as a transient period in his life, complicated by moving into a new house that he was doing up. In his description of his working day he came across as relaxed and content, perhaps not surprisingly in the context of having achieved the desirable time balance with their child, the benefit of two salaries and for each of them, a four-day working week.

Comparing fathers

These three fathers experienced fatherhood very differently, reflecting the particular contexts they found themselves in. Although they worked in similar jobs, they lived in very different societies – the organisations they worked for differed, together with the availability of informal (kin) support.

Bengt experienced pressure from being a father both at work and home, while Janez, with less responsibility for childcare, experienced the least pressure on his time. Chris (and his wife) were able, through flexible working arrangements, to synchronise their working time schedules and to achieve the 'right' balance of time with their baby.

Bengt, living in from Norway, was the least content. Norwegian parental leave, which is targeted at men, has not changed organisations' gendered notions of work commitment. Bengt was unusual in Norway as well as among most fathers in the study in that he took a more or less equal share of parental leave. However, he felt penalised by his private sector employer for doing so. His marriage was the most equalitarian in terms of sharing childcare and housework, but he appeared somewhat resentful of this. Interestingly he complained about his wife not pulling her weight with the child and at home. He also felt pressured by the time he needed to devote to house renovations and to studying. His solution was to turn to his own kin for help. This is a rather traditional solution in a modern equalitarian Scandinavian welfare state.

Chris, the Dutch father, was in the middle in terms of contentment. He felt somewhat pressed for time but, unlike Bengt, was able to accommodate his work so that he was still bringing in a full-time salary but working a compressed (four-day) week. Such working practices are common in the Netherlands, even in the private sector, and are found not only among parents with young children. In a society in which the domestic division of labour is still fairly traditional, Chris did not feel obliged to share the childcare and domestic work equitably with his wife. However, he was in sole charge of the child one day a week and was surprised to find he enjoyed it. Like Bengt, he had additional pressures; he was doing up their new house. On the other hand, unlike Bengt, he had less involvement with his son. The domestic work was shared but Chris mentioned his wife wanting to buy in domestic services to solve the time squeeze, a solution that was not seen as so acceptable in Norway. Indeed it was Chris's wife who appeared to be more hard-pressed than Chris, both at work and at home, while in Bengt's household, at least according to Bengt, he was the one who bore most of the brunt of the time squeeze.

Janez was the most content of the three – he was a relaxed, rather traditional father. He was able to commit himself fully to work as his wife took most of the childcare responsibility. He expressed no time pressure. In a society that has recently gone through an abrupt transition to a market economy, Janez focused on a sense of material achievement: having a job, a car, a wife, children and a house (all priorities for Janez). For Janez they were enough. Gender equality while on the horizon had not yet affected him and he seemed relieved. Fatherhood was less important now and he looked to the future when he expected it to become more important, that is, when the children progressed in their education. Grandparents currently occupy a more significant role in children's care in Slovenia in terms of everyday care and back-up support. It is interesting that both Janez and Chris depended on some childcare help from kin while Bengt also saw the solution to the time squeeze in these terms.

The conditions that emerge as supportive are different for fathers than for mothers. In the case of fathers with younger children (Chris and Bengt), issues of lack of synchronicity arose not only in relation to how they fitted their employment around family life – concern was expressed by Bengt and Chris about having to fit in the renovation of their houses, and in Bengt's case, the time he needed to spend on studying. Unlike in the mothers' cases, in the cases of Chris and Janez, support with childcare from their partners was to a great extent taken as given rather than sought after. Bengt, on the other hand, complained he did more than his share. Moreover, the father-friendly public/workplace policies available to two of the fathers were not entirely welcomed by them – Bengt did not wish to take long parental leave if he had another child while Chris complained that his entitlement to a four-day working week did not enable him to stay late at the office. Janez, who did not need to adjust his hours since his wife and her parents were the main carers of his children, did not seek to change his work conditions and was content with his ability to compartmentalise his work and family life.

Conclusion

In this chapter we have compared cases of parents in the same occupations – mothers at the lower end of the occupational status spectrum in the public sector and fathers at the upper end in the private sector. We have shown how social class and occupational status are necessary but not sufficient conditions influencing how these working parents experience their lives in the present. Low-status jobs in the public sector in some contexts offer a more supportive environment for mothers, although they may offer fewer rewards; for example, they may be more lenient about parents (mothers) taking time off or leave take-up. For fathers in higher-status jobs, employment and breadwinning continue to be central identities. This is less problematic in households where a traditional gender ideology is practised and accepted. In such cases the responsibility for and daily welfare of children remains typically the mother's concern. There are, of course, other cases where we might find different scenarios but we would need to look for the particularities and conditions that make for greater variation.

We have examined the resources and conditions that contribute to working parents' sense of wellbeing. Public policy and workplace support are important in making everyday life run smoothly, especially for mothers. However, other conditions are also important, particularly for mothers in low-status jobs: childcare support from the child's father, the availability of intergenerational family help, decent housing and affordable local childcare. Women's experiences of working and motherhood depend on the presence of one or more of these conditions, and Carol in the UK has none of these currently. For fathers these conditions appear to be less critical, especially if their partners shoulder most of the responsibility for childcare and domestic work. Compared with mothers, fathers have lower expectations of parenthood – the least content father was Bengt in Norway with its strong gender equity discourse, as he did the most childcare and household work. The most content father is Janez in Slovenia who did the least. Intergenerational help emerged as significant for all the parents. It compensated and substituted for lack of support from fathers, as in the cases of Dália and Janez. Even where little kin support was available and other support was significant, it was still important (for Susanne in Sweden and Bengt in Norway).

Those who viewed their lives more positively often compared themselves against the norm in a particular context. Thus the high-status fathers expressed little dissatisfaction in a context where it was accepted that childcare was women's responsibility. Those disadvantaged in the labour market (in this chapter the low-status mothers) compared themselves with those living in less fortunate circumstances (within the same context). Thus Rosa in Bulgaria counted herself 'lucky' compared with those of peers experiencing hardship. Carol, living in London, compared her lot unfavourably with others, unsurprisingly since she had little support from any source. However, it is also significant that earlier in her life she had high aspirations and in her current social context she lived amidst affluence.

A theme we have traced across all the cases is working parents' experience of time and the 'time squeeze'. The time squeeze may be understood in relation to changes in what it is to be a parent in contemporary society. It has been suggested that parenting has become a more intensive process (Fox, 2009; Hoffman, 2010), especially among middle-class families concerned to give their children the best possible start in life (Vincent and Ball, 2007). Intensive parenting is also a strategy that parents adopt to alleviate a variety of types of risk (Fox, 2009; Hoffman, 2010). In this framework of understanding, time for parenting becomes a contested issue, especially when both parents are working.

However, the causes of time pressure are themselves temporal. Feeling pressured by time arises through the simultaneity of the different domains in which lives are lived (Brose, 2004) and the extent to which this enables parents to synchronise the timings of different activities. These domains are constitutive of different meanings of time; in the work context chronological time may be important although work intensification and multitasking are dominant features of many jobs. Family time is fragmented and given meaning by parents and children's departure and coming home times, by meal times, by 'special times' or family time. Children's time frames are differentiated by day care and school timetables, by times to play and by the scheduling of extra-curricular activities. In addition parents' time frames include 'time for me', time for friends, time for study, time for household chores and household projects. Moreover, these domains often intersect, creating irreconcilable temporal experiences. The conditions of asynchronicity (Brose, 2004) and time acceleration (Rosa, 2007) are constitutive of working parents' current experience.

In most respects the case-based comparisons in this chapter echo the general findings of Chapter Six. However, they also add other dimensions to the understanding of parents' experiences. As discussed in Chapter Three, comparative case analysis can demonstrate what is unique in the biographies, current circumstances and experiences of particular individuals. At one level therefore, the cases of working mothers and fathers represent only themselves. Yet issues of generalisability beyond the cases arise both with respect to other similar cases in the study and beyond – to wider populations of working parents. However, generalisation can mean drawing theoretical as well empirical inferences. With respect to theoretical inferences we may extrapolate the feelings, conditions and resources that lead to or characterise particular outcomes such as contentment and time pressures. From a policy perspective, it is useful to see how particular policies and conditions work for particular individuals and how they pan out in seemingly similar conditions and across contexts. Thus it may be possible to see the nuances beneath general statistical generalisations and trends (nationally and internationally) and to explore the effects of public policy on the ground.

EIGHT

Conclusions

Suzan Lewis, Ann Nilsen and Julia Brannen

The chapters in this book have each contributed to a wider understanding of the transitions to and the experiences of parenthood across different European countries. The analysis of biographical cases was carried out taking account of a multilayered set of conditions: the nation state both over time and in the present; national institutions such as the system of education and welfare state provisions; gendered aspects of the labour market; and gendered expectations and practices across countries. In this final chapter we look at four key issues that are central to understanding the phenomenon of working parenthood that has been the focus of the book: the issue of time, including life course time and everyday time and, relatedly, the importance of context; the salience of class and gender; and finally we end with reflections about some implications for issues arising in the present and the future.

Life course and time

Different approaches to and perspectives on *time* is one of the overarching theoretical frameworks of this book. In much of what is current in sociological research, notions of modernity (late modernity, postmodernity and so forth) are employed to situate the present and to articulate historical change. The concept is applied to unspecified long-term trends and is commonly used in studies of family life and biographical research. In Chapter Two we outlined why we consider concepts of modernity and postmodernity too wide-ranging to be helpful for understanding a particular cohort's transitions to parenthood, as these take place in different national contexts. Instead we suggested that a life course perspective provides a better alternative. In this latter approach historical changes and continuities are foregrounded. Historical period does not refer to a loosely defined era but to particular periods of historical time. While, for example, late modernity sometimes refers to loosely defined places, for example, 'the Western world' in general, historical periods are discussed with reference to particular countries or regions. Hence a focus on a particular period offers the opportunity to contextualise biographical material and to discuss the transition to parenthood with reference to a multilayered spatial and diachronic framework that also encompasses specific (micro, meso and macro/national) contexts. This approach therefore captures the complexities of the agency–structure dynamic.

Biographical time is the notion that best describes the time that inscribes young people's trajectories to parenthood. By this we mean the timing and ordering of life course events and transitions such as leaving school, entry to the labour market, setting up an independent household and so forth. These dimensions are often discussed with reference to the transition between the life course phases of youth and adulthood that have been addressed at length in Chapters Four and Five. The timing and sequencing of transitions which lead to parenthood is set within historical time and the local and wider institutional context – the resources provided by families of origin, kin and by public policy and childcare in a particular country at particular moments in time. These pathways differ according to constraints and opportunity structures available. As has been suggested in the book, trajectories are formed in relation to a range of intersecting layers of context: education, occupation, family support and so on. What is considered a normative pathway to parenthood is variable depending on context and whether an individual is a mother or father and their social class trajectory, as shaped by education and occupation.

Time also inscribes parents' experiences of being a parent in the present. In Chapter Seven we adopted a temporal lens. We traced how a biographical event may continue to shape present experience. For example, separation from a partner may not only affect the resources parents can draw on to manage their work–family lives, depleting their family's material resources as well as childcare and housing, but they may also percolate parents' emotions producing feelings of dissatisfaction and low self-esteem. Indeed the life events of separation and divorce may be more salient in determining the experience of parenthood than other life course transitions. However, some national regimes of support for working parents will mitigate some of their consequences better than others, as in the case of Nordic welfare regimes.

Also in Chapter Seven, drawing on the notion of the simultaneity of events (Brose, 2004) in 'the world at reach' (Schutz and Luckmann, 1983), we suggested that parents occupy simultaneously different time domains, for example, in the realms of work time, family time, couple time, children's time and personal time. These different domains attract different meanings to time. For parents the collision of these different temporalities may result in an overwhelming sense of busyness and harriedness that pervades modern life (Gillis, 1996). As Warde (1999) suggests, the contemporary feeling of being 'squeezed' for time has less to do with shortage of time than with the issue of timing – a situation described by 'sociologists of time' as the problem of synchronisation. Parents have to solve the problems of synchronising what are often irreconcilable timetables. Such temporal pressures contribute to the daily experience of what it feels like to be a working parent.

Importance of context

The neglect of context, particularly although not exclusively in quantitative research, is increasingly noted in a range of disciplines. For example, Gephart (2004) observed the relative absence of qualitative context-rich research aimed explicitly at generating contextual theories (as opposed to contextualising quantitative research findings) in the management literature. Context is also frequently rendered invisible or unimportant in qualitative studies that are underpinned by social theories which foreground general notions of modernity as the main 'contextual' point of reference.

Research on work and parenthood too often neglects the surroundings in which these phenomena are played out, obscuring the interrelationships between structure and individual agency. One objective of the Transitions project was to gain an understanding of motherhood and fatherhood from a gendered, contextualised perspective across European states. We have seen in this book that men and women's experiences of the transition to parenthood and the day-to-day experience of being a working mother or father must be understood within these intersecting layers of society. The comparative case study design and the life course perspective adopted have highlighted the importance of the opportunity structures provided by different national institutional features for men and women from different social backgrounds in a particular historical period as they become parents and seek to manage their work and family lives.

Cross-national comparisons often focus solely on welfare state differences. As discussed in Chapter Three, the national level is approached in different ways in comparative research (Kohn, 1987), creating debates about what are the most appropriate foci for comparison (Brookes et al, 2011). As set out in Chapter Two, national context also encompasses broader institutional, economic, ideological and sociocultural conditions including, for example, education systems and family traditions. Research that relies only on one layer of context, for example, the macro level of public policy support, misses important variations in individual experiences and situated meanings. Our analysis has enabled us to tease out some of the particular conditions that shaped the lives of individual women and men in the transition to parenthood. We have shown how different layers of contexts, including public policies, employer practices, housing provisions, partner support, household and informal resources of different kinds, intersect and have an impact on parents' lives. Cross-national comparative studies can show how structural circumstances inform and affect individual life course trajectories, particularly the transition to motherhood and fatherhood.

However, while context is commonly neglected, particularly in quantitative research, specific aspects of it are not always articulated by interviewees. For example, as we saw in Chapter Four, the Norwegian welfare state is a very important source of support in the transition to parenthood yet it is not always acknowledged in the mothers' biographical accounts. Such support is often taken for granted, yet in other countries such as the UK and Portugal, parents have a lower sense of entitlement to support from the state (Lewis and Smithson, 2001) and expect more from their kin. The mixed method approach used in the wider Transitions project, which included a context-mapping exercise of public policies, provided a framework for analysing parents' biographical accounts and helped us to become more conscious of the 'taken-for-granted' aspects of context – the 'silent discourses' (Brannen and Nilsen, 2002) – and to bring them to bear in the discussion. National discourses and debates relating to working and parenting, among policy makers, employers and the media, were also analysed, providing a further crucial but often neglected backcloth which unfolded and shifted over the course of the project (Smithson and Lewis, 2003; Lewis and Smithson, 2006b). Together these data enabled us as researchers to contextualise the cases and interpret the similarities and differences between them with rigour and confidence.

In the wider project we also examined organisational contexts. Although the workplace has not been our main focus in this book, it clearly constitutes another important layer in understanding people's lives and the ways that parents experienced them. Workplaces are especially salient as parents in this study managed work and care in particularly intense, competitive and pressured workplaces marked by rapid organisational change, leading to increased workloads. The experience of work intensification and work pressure was found in all the organisations where the parents were employed (Lewis at al, 2009). At the same time work pressure was compounded by the way parenting is becoming a more intensive process (Fox, 2009; Hoffman, 2010) as parents in all countries are expected to put growing amounts of effort and time into parenting activities. This is particularly marked in middle-class families who invest considerable material resources in the 'cultivation' of the child (Vincent and Ball, 2007). As demonstrated in Chapter Seven, time for parenting, time for work and time for many other activities all compete with one another with the result that parents experience time pressure and have difficulty in reconciling these different temporalities.

Contexts are not static, but shift over time. We have explored transitions to parenthood within the institutional fabric of societies at a given historical time period. At the time of the Transitions study the most major economic and social changes were taking place in Bulgaria and Slovenia as their institutions adapted to the transition to a market economy, although there were differences in experiences and the rate of change between the two countries. We have seen, for example, how the shift from state-owned capital and generous state support to privatisation and cuts in state services underlined the importance of the wider family network for the generation of young parents in Bulgaria and Slovenia.

Salience of gender and class

Gender and social class are highly salient to the analysis of parents' lives, in particular for mothers, whose caregiving activities are often devalued. Labour markets and also systems of education are characterised by gender segregation across the national contexts, although to different degrees and in different forms. Families and workplaces are gendered in all countries in terms of occupational and sectoral segregation and also in terms of their policies and practices for employees. Even in countries with a strong ideological commitment to equality of opportunities and gender equity such as Sweden and Norway, the experiences of motherhood and fatherhood remain gendered, shaped by structural, cultural and practical factors. Our findings confirm that gender and class are still major factors that structure and shape the experiences of working and parenting across countries, as found in many other studies (see, for example, Lyness and Kropf, 2005; Crompton, 2010).

Gendered social structures thus represent yet another form of context that must be taken into consideration. Occupational segregation by gender follows sector divides in the economy: there are more women in public sector occupations in all countries and men dominate in the private sector.[1] Public sectors in most countries include caring and teaching, both female-dominated occupations (Lewis et al, 2009). There are many differences in conditions between those employed in public sector jobs in social services, and those with equivalent education levels who work in the private sector. The latter tend to have higher salaries while the former have higher job security (Crompton et al, 2003; Tronstad, 2007). However, these differences are also characterised by change and continuity. For example, public sector employment in the UK at the time of writing is no longer experienced as secure as it was at the time when the study was carried out.

A frequently recurring theme across the countries was the way in which gender shaped parenthood and made motherhood different from fatherhood both in everyday family life and in workplaces. The transition to parenthood is a critical 'tipping point' (Wiesmann et al, 2008). Even if couples negotiate a relatively equitable division of domestic labour prior to parenthood, once they become parents decisions are made, explicitly or implicitly, at the household level about who stays at home and for how long following children's births, and how to manage work and family demands. The biographical accounts and lifelines presented in Chapters Four and Five demonstrate how life course trajectories are gendered. Gaps for men in some countries are related to military service after upper secondary school and before higher education. Women, on the other hand, tend to have more periods of part-time work and longer leave periods following childbirth. Gender differences evident in the trajectories cannot be explained solely in terms of individual or household 'choices' although other research shows that mothers often rationalise their decision to work fewer hours, if the option is available, as a personal preference and trade-off under specific circumstances, knowing that it will disadvantage them (Webber and Williams, 2008; Lewis and Humbert, 2010). The choice discourse neglects the role of structural and relational factors, particularly gendered opportunity structures associated with institutional arrangements across national contexts (Brannen and Nilsen, 2005). Given that cases of lone parents figured in our material, we have seen both how lone parenthood is not a fixed state but also how being a lone parent may be different for a mother than a father and how important in some contexts is the support of kin (Portugal).

We suggested that socioeconomic status also strongly influences opportunity structures and supports and constraints for combining parenthood and employment. Social inequality remains a persistent aspect of European societies, although levels of social inequality differ across the countries studied (Fagnani et al, 2004). Indeed inequalities may be exacerbated by the growing gap between core and peripheral workforces. As the case analysis in Chapter Seven bears out, mothers in low-paid and low-status jobs, typically also partnered to men in similar work jobs, as well as lone parents in the same type of occupations are poorly resourced compared with two-income households in higher-status jobs. As demonstrated in Chapters Four and Five, social class is important for the transition to parenthood in all the countries in our study. However, the comparative analysis demonstrates that the impact of class must be considered within the overall resource situation relating to the institutional fabrics of different societies, while the combination of resources available to parents varies by the particularities of their situations.

Some of the 'choices' available to parents in more affluent countries, such as part-time work, often viewed as a resource, are simply not a possibility for parents in other contexts. However, as part-time working, where available, is overwhelmingly taken up by women and rarely associated with systemic workplace change, it can be a double-edged sword, providing a household strategy for working and parenting but also perpetuating gender inequalities in the home and the workplace. Gendered assumptions that ideal workers are those who conform to the male model of full-time work (Rapoport et al, 2002) stigmatise part-time workers and are one of the reasons for men's reluctance to reduce their working hours (along with a breadwinner ideology and economic considerations). These gendered assumptions about ideal workers may be more entrenched in some countries than others, but are nevertheless evident even in more equality-conscious Nordic countries (Ellingsæter, 2003; Holt and Lewis, 2012). The ideal worker norm is antithetical to motherhood ideologies that, in many contexts, prescribe that ideal mothers should not spend too much time at work, away from their children (Lewis, 1991; Ridgeway and Correll, 2004). Although motherhood ideologies vary across the countries, mothers are to some extent at least assumed to be the main carers everywhere. It is therefore not gender or class alone that disadvantages mothers but assumptions relating to their role as primary carers, as Ridgeway and Correll argue in the US (Ridgeway and Correll, 2004; Correll et al, 2007).

Ideologies of childcare, however, play out in different ways in different contexts. This relates not only to the assumed roles of mothers and fathers but also to the nature of provision available which in turn influences normative ideas about where support 'should' come from. Chapter Six, for example, highlights how childcare, the most basic and necessary support for working parents, is variously provided and hence viewed in different national contexts as a private, a family or a public concern. This variability has an impact on parents' childcare solutions and strategies, including working hours and feelings of entitlement to support.

Male breadwinner ideology and hence the assumed role of fathers appears to be changing to some extent across European societies, although at different rates and in different ways (Crompton et al, 2007). In our study, parents in several countries provided examples of men who took or wanted to take a bigger role in parenting, but felt constrained by organisational expectations and also by family and partner expectations. The gendered expectations of new fathers and mothers, as well as gendered organisational expectations, vary in the countries studied, but in every country mothers were more likely than fathers to take up the policies available for leave or flexible working.

Policies that address gender issues directly, such as the father's quota of parental leave, may be necessary for progress to occur towards gender-equitable parenting, but we found that they may also create tensions. This was illustrated by the case of Bengt, the Norwegian father discussed in Chapter Seven, who felt uneasy about his contributions at home and penalised by his private sector employer. In Norway and Sweden, where gender equality, including an ideal of shared parenting, is a public discourse, greater expectations can create transitional tensions as people adapt to new norms. Conflict is often in the form of mothers expecting more from their partners, but in the case of Bengt, he felt that he was doing too much and his wife was not pulling her weight. This illustrates the need for cyclical and reciprocal change in men and women's behaviours – as mothers change, fathers need to change too, requiring further change in mothers, and so on (Gambles et al, 2006).

In contrast, in Bulgaria gender equity in households was not a dominant discourse – other resources were available, namely childcare and grandparent care. Mothers in Bulgaria did not expect fathers to share parenting. There appeared, however, to be less tension in these households related to lower expectations of gender equity. As discussed in Chapter Six, expectations for managing work and family life may be more easily met in societies where ideals and expectations of gender equity are not yet widely established. This provokes questions about the ethics of raising expectations where this is unsettling. Equally, however, there are ethical issues in not raising expectations. Support from the extended family can ease young parents' burden but it can also absolve fathers from the need to change, and reproduce inequalities in the family. Negotiations between partners may create transitional tensions but may be a necessary step for social change in gender relations and greater equality. Changes within the family need to be reflected in other layers of context, notably workplace expectations.

Even in societies with a strong equality discourse and public policy that sustains gender equity, the ways that parents manage their work–

family lives depend on particular household projects and events. Men may invest more in the breadwinner role where the household deems it economically beneficial and/or where other resources are available to draw on. As the case analysis demonstrated, fathers may also 'choose' to use their time on household projects such as doing up houses (a major concern of men in the early family formation phase), or studying outside working hours to gain extra qualifications required to progress to a better job (see Chapter Seven).

Reflections on the present and looking to the future

The thick descriptions of cases in this book, set within multiple layers of context, provide an in-depth understanding of how social circumstances at different levels together form overarching frames of understanding for the unfolding of individual lives in the transition to parenthood and the day-to-day experiences of working parents. We have argued that cross-national, comparative case-based analyses can show how particular lives may be led if social conditions change and resources are differently distributed. In this section we consider how the cases discussed in this book might inform thinking about how to support parents as circumstances change over time. We first reflect on some of the dramatic changes that have occurred since the study took place, and how they may be altering layers of context and impinging on parents' experiences. We then consider how the cases may be helpful in thinking through implications of current and also future trends and scenarios for supporting and sustaining future generations of families, and provide an example to illustrate this. The major upheavals since the project was completed occurred at the global level – the global recession of 2008, exacerbated by the 2009 international banking crisis and its ongoing consequences. Although these crises affected the seven countries in different ways and to different extents, they nevertheless have potentially profound consequences for the circumstances in which people become parents and combine parenthood and employment, including economic, labour market, workplace and in some cases, public policy and housing across Europe.

Government responses to the needs of families in the economic crisis in the seven countries have varied. While some introduced additional (mainly temporary) measures to help families cope, others cut benefits and services to families such as childcare, housing benefits or tax credits (Gauthier, 2010). In some cases, families have been directly affected through job loss or a decline in income as a result of a reduction of their working hours (Gauthier, 2010), and there have been many more indirect effects. The effects of economic turbulence on parents' lives will depend very much on where they live.

In the final report to the EU on the Transitions project (Lewis and Smithson, 2006a), prior to the financial crises, we drew attention to some fundamental tensions between contemporary intensified working patterns and the needs of mothers and fathers to be able to care for children, as parents across Europe faced growing demands both in the workplace and the home. These tensions are likely to be heightened by the recession but it is also possible there could be some positive shifts for some parents in some cases. In Northern European countries, where part-time and flexible working arrangements are well developed, some employers are encouraging both men and women employees to reduce working times as a means of avoiding redundancy. While this will cause financial hardship for many, it could also create an opportunity for more equitable parenting opportunities. However, possible benefits will only occur where the income level is sufficient for families to manage on less than two full-time incomes and where there is cultural and practical support for gender equality over the working life course, particularly in the context of pensions crises and changes which are occurring in some countries (notably in the public sector, long a bastion of better pensions). Thus impacts will again depend on different layers of context.

Future scenarios and value of the case studies

It is likely that the need for national economies to maximise their workforces by ensuring that women and men can participate in and reach their potential in the world of work will continue as will the need for two incomes in most families. At the same time societies need to reproduce themselves and there is concern in many European states about low birth rates and the ageing of societies, particularly Portugal, Bulgaria and Slovenia in this study. Birth rates are lowest when it is most difficult to reconcile work and family and highest in the Nordic countries where conditions are relatively favourable for working families (Fagnani, 2007).

In the current difficult conditions that include decreasing state budgets across most of Europe (Gautier, 2010) there is a clear danger of family welfare taking second place to financial concerns. The UK is currently undergoing profound political, economic and social changes. The UK Coalition government that came into power in 2010 favours a massive reduction in the size of the state to reduce the national deficit (and for ideological reasons). Thus public sector employment has become very insecure. It is quite possible that some of those working in social services, such as the respondents in our study, will lose their jobs, and if not, workloads will certainly be even heavier as the workforce, but not the work demands, shrink. It is possible that employers may try to compensate for this difficult situation by offering more support to parents, but only if this has no financial cost. Morale is likely to be low in such workplaces and will continue to deteriorate. Parents will also be affected by cuts in state services and benefits such as child tax credits, rendering their lives even more precarious. We have seen how in Bulgaria, for example, cuts in state services led young parents to rely increasingly on the support of their kin for childcare and housing. Portugal now faces major economic problems that will have an impact, particularly on working mothers who work full time and bear most of the brunt of care.

When thinking about how to create possible interventions it is important to consider how positive change in parents' lives may come about through interventions at a number of levels. A rethink at the public policy at local, regional and national levels may begin to address some of the problems. Such a rethink relates to a central theme of the book, namely the life course perspective. A parent's life would be less fraught if they could spread their working time over the life course without financial penalty rather being forced back into the labour market full time when they become parents, especially single parents. Similarly, lives would be easier to manage if the time schedules of working and childcare were better synchronised.

Time policies have a long history in some European countries. Explicit time policies have been introduced in particular places including in Italy, France and Germany. It is argued that the Nordic countries practise implicit time policies in their mix of family, labour and gender policies which achieves a sort of 'time welfare' (Council of Europe, 2010). Interestingly, these policies derive from the concerns of urban planners relating to public space, transport and the distribution of services (Council of Europe, 2010). Time planning policies range from 'a more citizen-friendly organisation of services and opening hours (day care, libraries, public transport, citizen service centres) to the integration of user interests ("voice") in planning processes, the development of new urban development concepts such as dynamic construction permits and the integration of a time-plan into local land-use planning' (Council of Europe, 2010). These policy ideas are underpinned by Alain Supiot's idea of citizens having 'drawing rights' which cover those in non-marketable forms of work (the unemployed and non-employed) (see Bernier, 2006). Arguing against the choice rhetoric that underlies policies such as flexible working, Supiot's ideas are normative. They explicitly address the discontinuities of space and time, both life course and everyday time, making them directly relevant to the issues of this book and to how we can place those with caring responsibilities centre stage. Moreover, as Leisering (2003) suggests, life course policies should be 'life course sensitive', that is, they should reflect the previous life course patterns of recipients. They should also be 'life course relevant' in having an impact on the subsequent lives of recipients. Thus, with the reduction in pension entitlements and benefits life course policies, such as time savings accounts, should not have a negative impact on the provision people are able to make for their futures.

In this final chapter we have focused on five themes that have been central throughout the book. The first is *time* which is important not only when describing the transition to parenthood in which biographical time is at the forefront. We have also demonstrated the importance of historical time and everyday time in people's lives and their centrality to the theoretical and methodological frameworks employed in our analysis: the life course perspective and a biographical approach. Second, we have shown how different aspects and layers of *context* are integral to such an approach and to case analysis that requires 'thick descriptions': the more layers of context drawn on, the deeper the level of understanding and the higher the sociological relevance. The third topic is *gender and social class*: we have reiterated how social inequality continues to differentiate between the experiences of working parents. Fourth, we suggested how case material may be useful in *future scenario* thinking. Fifth, we highlighted the importance of developing policies at different levels of context, in particular noting the importance of time policies to the lives of working parents.

Note
[1] The size of the public sector differs between the countries. The Eastern European countries still have a high level of public sector employment as do Norway and Sweden (approximately 40 per cent); UK approximately 18 per cent, Portugal approximately 16 per cent and the Netherlands lowest, with 12 per cent (Hammouya, 1999; Handler et al, 2005).

References

Adam, B. (1995) *Time watch: The social analysis of time*, Cambridge: Polity Press.

Alwin, D.F. and McCammon, R.J. (2006) 'Generations, cohorts and social change', in J.T. Mortimer and M. Shanahan (eds) *Handbook of the life course*, New York: Springer, pp 23-49.

Anderson, P. (1998) *The origins of postmodernity*, London: Verso.

Anderson, P. (2009) *The new old world*, London: Verso.

Arts, W. and Gelissen, J. (2002) 'Three worlds of welfare capitalism or more? A state-of-the-art report', *Journal of European Social Policy*, vol 12, no 2, pp 137-58.

Bäck-Wiklund, M. and Plantin, L. (2005) 'The workplace as an arena for negotiating the work-family boundary: a case study of two Swedish social service agencies', in R. Crompton, S. Lewis and C. Lyonnette, *Women, men, work and family in Europe*, Basingstoke: Palgrave, pp 171-89.

Bailyn, L. (2006) *Breaking the mold: Redesigning work for productive and satisfying lives*, Cornell, NY: ILR Press.

Balchin, P. (1996) 'Introduction', in P. Balchin (ed) *Housing policy in Europe*, London: Routledge, pp 1-25.

Beck, U. and Beck-Gernsheim, E. (1995) *The normal chaos of love*, Cambridge: Polity Press.

Benson, J.E. and Furstenberg Jr, F.F. (2007) 'Entry into adulthood: are adult role transitions meaningful markers of adult identity?', *Advances in Life Course Research*, vol 11, pp 199-224.

Bernier, J. (2006) *Social protection for non standard workers outside the employment relationship*, Research for the Federal Labour Standards Review Commission.

Bertaux, D. (1990) 'Oral history approaches to an international social movement', in E. Øyen (ed) *Comparative methodology*, London: Sage Publications, pp 158-70.

Biggart, A. and Walther, A. (2006) 'Coping with yo-yo transitions. Young adults' struggle for support, between family and state in comparative perspective', in C. Leccardi and E. Ruspini (eds) *A new youth? Young people, generations and family life*, Aldershot: Ashgate, pp 41-62.

Billari, F.C. and Liefbroer, A.C. (2010) 'Towards a new pattern of transition to adulthood?', *Advances in Life Course Research*, vol 15, pp 59-75.

Bjerén, G. and Elgqvist-Saltzman, I. (eds) (1994) *Gender and education in a life perspective: Lessons from Scandinavia*, Avebury: Ashgate.

Blossfeld, H.-P. (2009) 'Comparative life course research. A cross-national and longitudinal perspective', in G. Elder and J. Giele (eds) *The craft of life course research*, New York: Guilford Press, pp 280-306.

Bonnell, V. and Hunt, L. (1999) 'Introduction', in V. Bonnell and L. Hunt (eds) *Beyond the cultural turn*, Berkeley, CA: University of California Press.

Bonoli, G. (1997) 'Classifying welfare states: a two-dimension approach', *Journal of Social Policy*, vol 26, no 3, pp 351-72.

Brandth, B. and Kvande, E. (2002) 'Reflexive fathers: negotiating parental leave and working life', *Gender, Work and Organisation*, vol 9, no 2, pp 186-203.

Brandth, B. and Kvande, E. (2003) *Fleksible fedre: Maskulinitet, arbeid, velferdsstat [Flexible fathers: Masculinity, work and the welfare state]*, Oslo: Universitetsforlaget.

Brannen, J. (2005a) 'Mixing methods: the entry of qualitative and quantitative approaches into the research process', *Social Research Methodology*, vol 8, no 3, pp 173-84.

Brannen, J. (2005b) 'Time and the negotiation of work-family boundaries: autonomy or illusion?', *Time and Society*, vol 14, pp 113-31.

Brannen, J. (2009) 'Working parenthood in a social service context: a UK case', in S.J. Lewis, J. Brannen and A. Nilsen (eds) *Work, families and organisations in transition: European perspectives*, Bristol: The Policy Press.

Brannen, J and M. Brockman (2005) 'Transitions UK Interview report', London: Institute of Education (unpublished).

Brannen J. and Nilsen, A. (2002) 'Young people's time perspectives: from youth to adulthood', *Sociology*, vol 36, no 3, pp 513-38.

Brannen, J. and Nilsen, A. (2005) 'Individualisation, choice and structure: a discussion of current trends in sociological analysis', *The Sociological Review*, vol 53, no 3, pp 412-28.

Brannen, J. and Nilsen, A. (2006) 'From fatherhood to fathering: transmission and change among British fathers in four-generation families', *Sociology*, vol 40, no 2, pp 335-52.

Brannen, J., Moss, P. and Mooney, A. (2004) *Working and caring over the twentieth century: Change and continuity in four-generation families*, ESRC Future of Work Series, Basingstoke: Palgrave Macmillan.

Brannen, J., Lewis, S., Nilsen, A. and Smithson, J. (eds) (2002) *Young Europeans, work and family: Futures in transition*, London: Routledge.

Brayfield, A. (1995) 'Juggling jobs and kids: the impact of employment schedules on fathers caring for children', *Journal of Marriage and the Family*, vol 57, May, pp 321-32.

Brookes, M., Croucher, R., Fenton-O'Creevy, M. and Gooderham, P. (2011) 'Measuring competing explanations of human resource management practices through the Cranet Survey: cultural versus institutional explanations', *Human Resource Management Review*, vol 21, no 1, pp 68-79.

Brose, H. (2004) 'An introduction towards a culture of simultaneity', *Time and Society*, vol 13, pp 5-26.

Buchman, M. (1989) *The script of life in modern society: Entry into adulthood in a changing world*, Chicago, IL: University of Chicago Press.

Cain, L. (1964) 'Life course and social structure', in R.E.L. Faris (ed) *Handbook of modern sociology*, Chicago, IL: Rand McNully et co, pp 272-309.

Callan, S. (2007 'Implications of family-friendly policies for organizational culture: findings from two case studies', Work, Employment and Society, vol 21, no 4, pp 673-91.

Černigoj Sadar, N. and Kersnik P. (eds) (2005) *Well-being in young European adults negotiating the work–family boundary*, Transitions Research Report #10 for the EU Framework 5 funded study 'Gender, parenthood and the changing European workplace', Manchester: Research Institute for Health and Social Change, Manchester Metropolitan University.

Christensen, T. and Lægreid, P. (eds) (2007) *Transcending new public management: The transformation of public sector reforms*, Aldershot: Ashgate.

Coltrane, S. (1996) *Family man: Fatherhood, housework, and gender equity*, New York: Oxford University Press.

Correll, S.J., Benard, B. and Paik, I. (2007) 'Getting a job. Is there a motherhood penalty?', *American Journal of Sociology*, pp 1297-338.

Council of Europe (2010) *Social time, leisure time: Which local time planning policy?*, CPL (19)3, 22 September, Paris: The Congress of Local and Regional Authorities: The voice of Cities and Regions.

Crompton, R. (1999) *Restructuring gender relations and employment: The decline of the male breadwinner*, Cambridge: Cambridge University Press.

Crompton, R. (2010) 'Class and employment', *Work, Employment and Society*, vol 24, no 1, pp 9-26.

Crompton, R., Dennett, J. and Wigfield, A. (2003) *Organisations, careers and caring*, Bristol: The Policy Press.

Crompton, R., Lewis, S. and Lyonette, C. (eds) (2007) *Women, men, work and family in Europe*, Basingstoke: Palgrave.

Daly, M. and Rake, K. (2003) *Gender and the welfare state: Care, work and welfare in Europe and the USA*, Cambridge: Polity Press.

das Dores Guerreiro, M., Abrantes, P. and Pereira, I. (2004) *Gender, parenthood and the changing European workplace*, Transitions Research Report #3, Case studies report for the EU Framework 5 funded study, Manchester: Research Institute for Health and Social Change, Manchester Metropolitan University.

das Dores Guerreiro, M., Abrantes, P. and Pereira, I. (2009) 'Changing contexts, enduring roles? Working parents in Portuguese public and private sector organisations', in Lewis, S., Brannen, J. and Nilsen, A. (eds) *Work, families and organisations in transitions. European perspectives*, Bristol: The Policy Press pp 149-66.

das Dores Guerreiro, M., Pereira Cardoso, I. and Abrantes, P. (2005) *Portuguese interview study report*, Lisbon University Institute (ISCTE).

Deacon, B. (2000) 'Eastern European welfare states: the impact of the politics of globalisation', *Journal of European Social Policy*, vol 10, no 2, pp 146-61.

de Almeida, A.N., das Dores Guerreiro, M., Lobo, C., Torres, A. and Wall, K. (2000) 'Family relations: change and diversity', in J.M.L. Viegas and A.F. da Costa, *Crossroads to modernity. Contemporary Portuguese society*, Oeiras: Celta editora, pp 41-70.

den Dulk, L., Peper, B. and van Doorne-Huiskes, A. (2003) *Literature review. Consolidated report*, Manchester: Manchester Metropolitan University.

den Dulk, L., Peper, B., Černigoj Sadar, N., Lewis, S., Smithson, J. and van Doorne-Huiskes, A. (2011) 'Work, family and managerial attitudes and practices in the European workplace: comparing Dutch, British and Slovenian financial sector managers', *Social Politics*, vol 18, no 2, pp 300-29.

Denzin, N. (1989) *Interpretive biography*, Qualitative Research Methods Series 17, London: Sage Publications.

Dermott, E. (2008) *Intimate fatherhood: A sociological analysis*, London: Routledge.

Duyvendak, J.W. and Stavenuiter, M. (2004) *Working fathers, caring men*, Utrecht: Verwey-Jonker institute.

Edwards, R., Doucet, A. and Furstenberg, F. (2009) 'Fathering across diversity and adversity: international perspectives and policy interventions', Special issue, *The Annals of the American Association of Political and Social Sciences*, vol 624, no 1.

Elder, G. (1985) 'Perspectives on the life course', in G. Elder (ed) *Life-course dynamics: Trajectories and transitions 1968-1980*, Ithaca, NY and London: Cornell University Press.

Elder, G. (1999 [1974]) *Children of the Great Depression. Social change in life experience*, Oxford: Westview Press.

Elder, G., Johnson, M.K. and Crosnoe, R. (2006) 'The emergence and development of life course research', in J.T. Mortimer and M. Shanahan (eds) *Handbook of the life course*, NewYork: Springer, pp 3-22.

Ellingsæter, A.L. (2003) 'The complexity of family policy reform: the case of Norway', *European Societies*, vol 5, no 4, pp 419-43.

Ellingsæter, A.L. and Leira, A. (eds) (2004) *Velferdsstaten og familien [The welfare state and the family]*, Oslo: Gyldendal.

Ellingsæter, A.L. and Solheim, J. (eds) (2002) *Den usynlige hånd. Kjønnsmakt og det moderne arbeidsliv [The invisible hand: Gender, power and the modern working life]*, Oslo: Gyldedal Akademisk.

Ellingsæter, A.L., Noack, T. and Rønsen, M. (1997) 'Sosial ulikhet blant kvinner: Polarisering, utjevning eller status quo?', *Tidsskrift for samfunnsforskning [Journal of Social Research]*, vol 1, pp 33-69. .

Esping-Andersen, G. (1990) *Three worlds of welfare capitalism*, Princeton, NJ: Princeton University Press.

ESS (European Social Survey) (2010) *ESS Round 4* (www. europeansocialsurvey.org/).

Eurostat (2009) *Youth in Europe.A statistical portrait* (http://epp.eurostat. ec.europa.eu).

Fagan, C. and Walthery, P. (2011) 'Individual working-time adjustments between full-time and part-time working in European firms'. *Social Politics: International Studies in Gender, State and Society*, vol 18, no 2, pp 269-99.

Fagan, C., Hegewisch, A. and Pillinger, J. (2006) *Out of time.Why Britain needs a new approach to working-time flexibility*, TUC Research Paper, London: Trades Union Congress.

Fagnani, J.G. (2007) 'Fertility rates and mothers' employment behaviour in comparative perspective: similarities and differences in six European countries', in R. Crompton, S. Lewis and C. Lyonette (eds) *Women, men, work and family in Europe*, Basingstoke: Palgrave.

Fagnani, J.G., Houriet-Ségard, G. and Bédouin, S. (2004) *Context mapping for the EU Framework 5 funded study, Gender, parenthood and the changing European workplace*, Transitions Research Report #1, Manchester: Research Institute for Health and Social Change, Manchester Metropolitan University.

Ferrera, M. (1996) 'The "southern model" of welfare in social Europe', *Journal of European Social Policy*, vol 6, no 1, pp 17-37.

Fox, B. (2009) *When couples become parents: The creation of gender in the transition to parenthood*, Toronto: University of Toronto Press.

Försäkringskassan (2010) *Försäkringsanalys, föräldraförsäkringen* ['Swedish Social Insurance'] (www.forsakringskassan.se).

Gambles, R., Lewis, S. and Rapoport, R. (2006) *The myth of work–life balance. The challenge of our time. Men, women, and societies*, Chichester: Wiley.

Gauthier, A.H. (2010) *The impact of the economic crisis on family policies in the European Union*. Brussels: European Commission.

Geertz, C. (2000 [1973]) *The interpretation of cultures. Selected essays*, New York: Basic Books.

Gephart, R. (2004) 'Qualitative research and the *Academy of Management Journal*', *Academy of Management Journal*, vol 47, pp 454-62.

Gillis, J. R. (1996) *A world of their own making: Myth, ritual and the quest for family values*, New York: Basic Books

Gobo, G. (2008) 'Re-conceptualising generalisation: old ideas in a new frame', in J. Aluusatari, L. Brannen and L. Bickman (eds) *Handbook of social research*, London: Sage Publications, pp 193-213.

Gomm, R., Hammersley, M. and Foster, P. (2000) 'Case study and generalisation', in R. Gomm, M. Hammersley and P. Foster (eds) *Case study method*, London: Sage Publications, pp 98-115.

Haas, L. and Hwang, P. (2007) 'Gender and organizational culture. Correlates of companies' responsiveness to fathers in Sweden', Gender and Society, vol 21, no 1, pp 52-79.

Haas, L. and Hwang, P. (2009) 'Is fatherhood becoming more visible at work? Trends in corporate support for fathers taking parental leave in Sweden', *Fathering*, vol 7, no 3, pp 303-321.

Hammersley, M. (2008) *Questioning qualitative inquiry. Critical essays*, London: Sage Publications.

Hammersley, M. and Gomm, R. (2008) 'Introduction', in R. Gomm, M. Hammersley and P. Foster (eds) *Case study method*, London: Sage Publications, pp 1-16.

Hammouya, M. (1999) 'Statistics on public sector employment: methodology, structures and trends', Working Papers, Geneva: ILO Sectorial Activities Programme Bureau of Statistics.

Handler, H., Koebel, B., Reiss, P. and Schratzenstaller, M. (2005) *The size and performance of public sector activities in Europe*, WIFO Working Paper 246, Vienna: Austrian Institute of Economic Research.

Hantrais, L. (2009) *International comparative research. Theory, methods and practice*, Basingstoke: Palgrave Macmillan.

Hareven, T.K. (1978) 'The last stage: historical adulthood and old age', in E. Erikson (ed) *Adulthood*, New York: Norton & Co, pp 201-15.

Hareven, T.K. (1982) *Family time and industrial time. The relationship between the family and work in a New England industrial community*, Cambridge: Cambridge University Press.

Hartmann, D. and Swartz, T.T. (2007) 'The new adulthood? The transition to adulthood from the perspective of transiting young adults', *Advances in Life Course Research*, vol 11, pp 253-86.

Harvey, D. (2003) *The new imperialism*, Oxford: Oxford University Press.

Heinz, W., Huinink, J., Swader, C.S. and Weyman, A. (2009) 'General introduction', in W. Heinz, J. Huinink, C.S. Swader and A. Weyman (eds) *The life course reader*, Frankfurt/Main: Campus Verlag, pp 15-30.

Hobsbawm, E. (1994) *Age of extremes. The short 20th century 1914-1991*, London: Michael Joseph.

Hobson, B. and Fahlen, S. (2009) 'Competing scenarios for European fathers: applying Sen's agency and capabilities framework to work–life balance', *Annals of the American Academy of Political and Social Science*, vol 64, pp 214-43.

Hobson, B. and Morgan, D. (2002) 'Introduction', in B. Hobso (ed) *Making men into fathers: Masculinities and the social politics of fatherhood*, Cambridge: Cambridge University Press.

Hochschild, A. (1997) *The time bind: When home becomes work and work becomes home*, Berkeley, CA: Henry Holt & Co.

Hoffman, D. (2010) 'Risky investment: parenting and the production of the "resilient child"', *Health, Risk and Society*, vol 12, no 4, pp 385-94.

Holt, H. and Lewis, S. (2012: in press) '"You can stand on your head and you still end up with lower pay": gendered work practices in two Danish workplaces', *Gender, Work and Organisation* [first published online in 2009 at http://onlinelibrary.wiley.com/doi/10.1111/j.1468-0432.2009.00501.x/abstract].

Holter, H. (1984) 'Women's research and social theory', in H. Holter (ed) *Patriarchy in a welfare society*, Oslo: Universitetsforlaget, pp 9-25.

Irwin, S. (1995). *Rights of passage: Social change and the transition from youth to adulthood*, London: UCL Press.

ISSP (International Social Survey Programme) (1998) (www.Issp.org).

Jones, G. and Wallace, C. (1992) *Youth, family and citizenship*, Buckingham: Open University Press.

Jordan, W. (1978) 'Searching for adulthood in America', in E. Erikson (ed) *Adulthood*, New York: Norton & Co, pp 189-99.

Kalleberg, A.L. (2000) 'Nonstandard employment relations: part-time, temporary and contract work', *Annual Review of Sociology*, vol 26, pp 341-65.

Knudsen, K. and Waerness, K. (2008) 'National context and spouses' housework in 34 countries', *European Sociological Review*, vol 24, no 1, pp 97-113.

Kohli, M. (1981) 'Biography: account, text, method', in D. Bertaux (ed) *Biography and society*, London: Sage Publications, pp 61-75.

Kohli, M. (2009) 'The world we forgot: a historical review of the life course', in W. Heinz, J. Huinink, C.S. Swader and A. Weyman (eds) *The life course reader*, Frankfurt/Main: Campus Verlag, pp 64-90.

Kohn, M.L. (1987) 'Cross-national research as an analytic strategy: American Sociological Association 1987 presidential address', *American Sociological Review*, vol 52, no 6, pp 713-31.

Kovacheva, S. (2000) *Sinking or swimming in the waves of transformation? Young people and social protection in Central and Eastern Europe*, Brussels: Youth Forum.

Kovacheva, S. (2001) 'Flexibilisation of youth transitions in Central and Eastern Europe', *YOUNG*, vol 9, no 1, pp 41-60.

Kovacheva, S. (2009) 'Organisational social capital and its role in the support of working parents: the case of a public social assistance agency in Bulgaria', in S. Lewis, J. Brannen and A. Nilsen (eds) *Work, families and organisations in transition: European perspectives*, Bristol: The Policy Press, pp 63-80.

Kovacheva, S. (2010) *Work–life balance: Young working parents between opportunities and constraints*, Sofia: East-West.

Kovacheva, S. and Matev, A. (2005) *Bulgarian national interview report*, Plovdiv, Bulgaria: University of Plovdiv.

Kovacheva, S., Matev, A. and Demira, N. (2004) 'Transitions: Organisational case studies – Bulgaria', unpublished, Plovdiv: Plovdiv University.

Lamb, M.E. and Lewis, C. (2004) 'The development and significance of father–child relationships in two-parent families', in M.E. Lamb (ed) *The role of the father in child development* (4th edn), Chichester: Wiley, pp 272-307.

Lappegård, T. (1999) 'Akademikere får også barn, bare senere', *Samfunnsspeilet*, nr 5 (www.ssb.no/samfunnsspeilet/). (Academics have children too, only later in *Society Reflected*)

Lareau, A. and Weininger, E. (2008) 'Class and the transition to adulthood', in A. Lareau and D. Conley (eds) *Social class. How does it work?*, New York: Russell Sage Foundation.

Leisering, L. (2003) 'Government and the life course', in J. Mortimer and M. Shanahan (eds) *Handbook of social research*, New York: Kluwer Academic/Plenum Publishers.

Lewis, J. (2001) 'The decline of the male breadwinner model: implications for work and care', *Social Politics*, vol 8, no 2, pp 152-69.

Lewis, J. (2006) 'Work/family reconciliation, equal opportunities and social policies: the interpretation of policy trajectories at the EU level and the meaning of gender equality', *Journal of European Public Policy*, vol 13, no 3, pp 420-37.

Lewis, J., Knijn, T., Martin, C. and Ostner, I. (2008) 'Patterns of development in work/family reconciliation policies for parents in France, Germany, The Netherlands and the UK in the 2000s', *Social Politics*, vol 15, no 3, pp 261-86.

Lewis, S. (1991) 'Motherhood and/or employment', in A. Phoenix, A. Woollett and E. Lloyd (eds) *Motherhood: Meanings, practices and ideologies*, London: Sage Publications.

Lewis, S. and Cooper, C. (2005) *Work–family integration: Case studies of organisational change*, London: Wiley.

Lewis, S. and Humbert, A. (2010) 'Discourse or reality? "Work–life balance", flexible working policies and gendered organisations', *Equal Opportunities International*, vol 29, pp 239-54.

Lewis, S. and Smithson, J. (2001) 'Sense of entitlement to support for the reconciliation of employment and family life', *Human Relations*, vol 54, pp 1455-81.

Lewis, S. and Smithson, J. (2006a) *Final report on the project 'Gender, Parenthood and the Changing European Workplace: Young Adults Negotiating the Work–Family Boundary': Transitions*, Manchester: Manchester Metropolitan University.

Lewis, S. and Smithson, J. (2006b) 'National debates on the reconciliation of paid work and family life: a research note', in L. den Dulk, T. van der Lippe and J. Schippers (eds) *Emancipatie als kwestie. Liber Amicorum voor Anneke van Doorne-Huiskes rond het thema vrouwen en beroepsparticipatie*, Amsterdam: Dutch University Press, pp 211-24.

Lewis, S., Brannen, J. and Nilsen, A. (eds) (2009) *Work, families and organisations in transition: European perspectives*, Bristol: The Policy Press.

Lewis, S., Gambles, R. and Rapoport, R. (2007) 'The constraints of a work–life balance approach. An international perspective', *International Journal of Human Resource Management*, vol 18, no 3, pp 360-73.

Lincoln, Y. and Guba, E. (1985) *Naturalistic inquiry*, Beverley Hills, CA: Sage Publications.

Loewenberg, P. (1971) 'The psychohistorical origins of the Nazi youth cohort', *The American Historical Review*, vol 76, no 5, pp 1457-502.

Lyness, K. and Kropf, K.B. (2005) 'The relationships of national gender equality and organizational support with work–family balance: a study of European managers', *Human Relations*, vol 58, no 1, pp 33-60.

Machado, F.L. and da Costa, A.F. (2000) 'An incomplete modernity', in J.M.L. Viegas and A.F. da Costa, *Crossroads to modernity. Contemporary Portuguese society*, Oeiras: Celta editora, pp 15-40.

Mannheim, K. (1952) 'The problem of generations', in K. Mannheim and P. Kecskemeti (eds) *Essays on the sociology of knowledge*, London: Routledge and Kegan Paul, pp 276-320.

Mills, C.W. (1963 [1940]) 'Situated actions and vocabularies of motive', in I.L. Horowitz (ed) *Power, politics and people. The collected essays of C. Wright Mills*, Oxford: Oxford University Press, pp. 439-452.

Mills, C.W. (1980 [1959]) *The sociological imagination*, London: Penguin.

Mitev, P.-E. (ed) (2005) *The new young. Bulgarian youth and the European perspective*, Sofia: East-West.

Mjøset, L. (2007) 'No fear of comparison or context: on the foundations of historical sociology', *Comparative Education*, vol 42, pp 337-62.

Moen, P. (2011) 'From work–family to gendered life course and "fit": five challenges to the field', *Community, Work and Family*, vol 14, no 1, pp 81-97.

Molyneux, M. (1991) 'The "women question" in the age of perestroika', *Agenda*, no 10, pp 89-108.

Mrcela, A.K. (2008) 'Men and women balancing work and life in transition:"cool modern" or "warm modern" model?', in S. Kovacheva (ed) 'Work–life dilemmas: Changes in work and family life in the enlarged Europe', *Sociological Problems*, Special Issue, vol IL, pp 174-92.

Nilsen, A. (1994) 'Life lines – a methodological approach', in G. Bjerén and I. Elgqvist-Saltzman (eds) *Gender and education in a life perspective: Lessons from Scandinavia*, Avebury: Ashgate, pp 101-15.

Nilsen, A. (1996) 'Stories of life – stories of living: women's narratives and feminist biography', *NORA, Nordic Journal of Women's Studies*, vol 4, no 1, pp 16-30.

Nilsen, A. (2011) 'Work, life course and gender: career and non–career jobs in context', *European Societies* (http://dx.doi.org/10.1080/146 16696.2010.547943).

Nilsen, A. and Brannen, J. (2002) 'Theorising the individual-structure dynamic', in J. Brannen, S. Lewis, A. Nilsen and J. Smithson (eds) *Young Europeans, work and family: Futures in transition*, London: Routledge, pp 30-47.

Nilsen, A. and Brannen, J. (2005) *Interview study consolidated report for the EU framework 5 funded study: Gender, Parenthood and the Changing European Workplace*, Transitions Report #8, Manchester: Manchester Metropolitan University.

Nilsen, A. and Brannen, J. (2010) 'The use of mixed methods in biographical research', in A. Tashakkori and C. Teddlie (eds) *SAGE handbook of mixed methods in social and behavioural research* (2nd edn), Los Angeles, CA: Sage Publications, pp 677-96.

Nilsen, A., das Dores Guerreira, M. and Brannen, J. (2002) '"Most choices involve money": different pathways to adulthood', in J. Brannen, S. Lewis, A. Nilsen and J. Smithson (eds) *Young Europeans, work and family: Futures in transition*, London: Routledge, pp 162-84.

Nilsen, A., Sümer, S. and Granlund, L. (2009) 'Parents and organisational change: a cross-sector comparison of two Norwegian organisations', in S. Lewis, J. Brannen and A. Nilsen (eds) *Work, families and organisations in transition: European perspectives*, Bristol: The Policy Press, pp 131-48.

OECD (Organisation for Economic Co-operation and Development) (2008) *Education at a glance. OECD indicators* (www.oecd.org).

OECD (2010) *Education at a glance. OECD indicators* (www.oecd.org).

Ollier-Malaterre, A. (2010) 'Contributions of work–life and resilience initiatives to the individual/organization relationship', *Human Relations*, vol 63, no 1, pp 41-62.

Pascall, G. and Kwak, A. (2005) *Gender regimes in transitions in Central and Eastern Europe*, Bristol: The Policy Press.

Plantin, L. (2007) 'Different classes, different fathers? On fatherhood, economic conditions and class in Sweden', *Community, Work and Family*, vol 10, no 1, pp 93-110.

Plantin, L. and Bäck-Wiklund, M. (2009) 'Social service as human service: between loyalties. A Swedish case', in S. Lewis, J. Brannen and A. Nilsen (eds) *Work, families and organisations in transition: European perspectives*, Bristol: The Policy Press, pp 49-62.

Plantin, L., Månsson, S.-A. and Kearney, J. (2003) 'Talking and doing fatherhood. On fatherhood and masculinity in Sweden and Britain', *Fathering*, vol 1, no 1, pp 3-26.

Pollert, A. (2003) 'Women, work and equal opportunities in post-communist transition', *Work, Employment and Society*, vol 17, no 2, pp 331-57.

Rapoport, R., Bailyn, L., Fletcher, J.K. and Pruitt, B.H. (2002) *Beyond work-family balance: Advancing gender equity and workplace performance*, London: Jossey Bass.

Ridgeway, C.L. and Corell, S.J. (2004) 'Motherhood as a status characteristic', *Journal of Social Issues*, vol 60, no 4, pp 683-700.

Riley, M.W. (ed) (1988) *Social structures and human lives*, Newbury Park, CA: Sage Publications.

Roberts, K. (2006) 'Young people and family life in Eastern Europe', in C. Leccardi and E. Ruspini (eds) *A new youth? Young people, generations and family life*, Aldershot: Ashgate, pp 203-21.

Roberts, K. (2009) *Youth in transition. Eastern Europe and the West*, Basingstoke: Palgrave Macmillan.

Rosa, H. (ed) (2009) *High-speed society: Social acceleration, power and modernity*, University Park, PA: Pennsylvania State University Press.

Ryder, N. (1965) 'The cohort as a concept of social change', *American Sociological Review*, vol 30, pp 843-61.

Samuel, N. (1985) 'Is there a distinct cross-national comparative sociology, method and methodology?', *Cross-National Research Papers*, vol 1, no 1, pp 3-10.

Savage, M. and Burrows, R. (2009) 'Some further reflections on the coming crisis of empirical sociology', *Sociology*, vol 43, no 4, pp 762-74.

SCB (Statistics Sweden) (2009) Tabell over *Sveriges befolkning* nr 2.2.11. 'Moderns och faderns ålder vid första, andra och tredje barnet' [Table from 'The Swedish population', 2.2.11. 'The age of the mother and father at their first, second and third child'] (www.scb.se).

Schofield, J.W. (2000) 'Increasing the generalizability of qualitative research', in R. Gomm, M. Hammersley and P. Foster (eds) *Case study method*, London: Sage Publications, pp 69-97.

Schutz, A. and Luckmann, T. (1983) *The structures of the life-world*, Evanston, IL: Northwestern University Press.

Sebastião, J. (2000) 'The dilemmas of education. Universality, diversity and innovation', in J.M.L. Viegas and A.F. da Costa, *Crossroads to modernity. Contemporary Portuguese society*, Oeiras: Celta editora, pp 261-78.

Sennett, R. (1998) *The corrosion of character. The personal consequences of work in the new capitalism*, New York: W.W. Norton.

Settersten, R.A. (2004) 'Age structuring and the rhythm of the life course', in J. Mortimer and M. Shananhan (eds) *Handbook of the life course*, New York: Kluwer Academic/Plenum Publishers, pp. 81-102.

Settersten, R.A. (2009) 'It takes two to tango: the (un)east dance between life-course sociology and life-span psychology', *Advances in Life Course Research*, vol 14, pp 74-81.

Settersten, R.A. and Hagestad, G. (1996a) 'What's the latest? Cultural age deadlines for family transitions', *The Gerontologist*, vol 36, no 2, pp 178-88.

Settersten, R.A. and Hagestad, G. (1996b) 'What's the latest? II. Cultural age deadlines for educational and work transitions', *The Gerontologist*, vol 36, no 5, pp 602-13.

Settersten, R.A. and Mayer, K.U. (1997) 'The measurement of age, age structuring, and the life course', *Annual Review of Sociology*, vol 23, pp 233-61.

Smithson, J. and Lewis, S. (2003) *Consolidated report on national discourses and debates*. Transitions, Manchester: Research Institute for Health and Social Change, Manchester Metropolitan University.

Smithson, J. and S. Lewis (2005) 'The psychological contract and work-family', *Organization Management Journal*, vol 1, no 1, pp 70-81.

Southerton, D. (2003) 'Squeezing time': allocating practices, coordinating networks and scheduling society, *Time & Society*, vol 12, no 1, pp 5-25.

Stafseng, O. (1996) *Den historiske konstruksjon av moderne ungdom* [*The historical construction of modern youth*], Oslo: Cappelen Akademiske Forlag.

Stake, R. E. (2000) 'The case study method in social inquiry', in Gomm, R., Hammersley, M. and Foster, P. *Case Study Method,* London: Sage, pp 19-26.

Stauber, B. (2006) 'Biography and gender in youth transitions', in M. du Bois-Reymond and L. Chisholm (eds) *The modernisation of youth transitions in Europe,* Wiley Periodicals, no 113, Fall, pp 63-76.

Stoilova, R. (2001) *Inequalities and community integration,* Sofia: LIK.

Sümer, S. (2009) *European gender regimes and policies. Comparative perspectives.* Farnham: Ashgate Publishing.

Syltevik, L.J. (2007) 'Taking control of one's own life? Norwegian lone mothers experiencing the new employment strategy', *Community, Work & Family,* vol 9, no 1, pp 75-94.

Thomas, W.I. and Znaniecki, F. (1958 [1918-20]) *The Polish peasant in Europe and America. Vol 1-2,* New York: Dover.

Tronstad, K.R. (2007) *Fordelingen av økonomiske ressurser melom kvinner og menn: Inntekt, sysselsetting og tidsbruk* [*The distribution of economic resources between women and men: Income, employment and time use*], Oslo: Central Bureau of Statistics.

Ungdomsstyrelsen (2003) *Dom kallar oss unga,* Stockholm: Ungdomsstyrelsen. Youth department (2003) *They call us young people.*

Vincent, C. and Ball, S. (2007) '"Making up" the middle class: families, activities and class dispositions', *Sociology,* vol 41, no 6, pp 1061-77.

Wærness, K. (1982) *Kvinneperspektiver på sosialpolitikken* [*Women's perspectives on social policy*], Oslo: Universitetsforlaget.

Wallace, C. and Kovacheva, S. (1998) *Youth in society. The construction and deconstruction of youth in East and West Europe,* London and New York: Macmillan and St Martin's Press.

Warde, A. (1999) 'Convenient food: space and timing', *British Food Journal,* vol 101, no 7, pp 518-27.

Webber, C. and Williams, C. (2008) 'Mothers in "good" and "bad" part time jobs', *Gender and Society,* vol 22, pp 752-77.

Wengraf, T. (2001) *Qualitative research interviewing,* London: Sage Publications.

Wiesmann, S.M., Boeije, H.R., van Doorne-Huiskes, A. and den Dulk, L. (2008) 'Not worth mentioning: implicit and explicit nature of decision-making about the division of paid and domestic work', *Community, Work & Family*, vol 1, no 4, pp 341-63.

Yin, R.K. (2003) *Case study research. Design and methods* (3rd edn), London: Sage Publications.

Index